Devrim F. Kilicer

Tower Power:
The US on a Freudian Couch after 9/11

A Socio-Psychoanalytic Study of New York Towers

Devrim F. Kilicer

TOWER POWER:
THE US ON A FREUDIAN COUCH AFTER 9/11

A Socio-Psychoanalytic Study of New York Towers

ibidem-Verlag
Stuttgart

Bibliografische Information der Deutschen Nationalbibliothek
Die Deutsche Nationalbibliothek verzeichnet diese Publikation in der
Deutschen Nationalbibliografie; detaillierte bibliografische Daten sind im
Internet über http://dnb.d-nb.de abrufbar.

Bibliographic information published by the Deutsche Nationalbibliothek
Die Deutsche Nationalbibliothek lists this publication in the Deutsche Nationalbibliografie;
detailed bibliographic data are available in the Internet at http://dnb.d-nb.de.

Cover picture: © Papillon/PIXELIO

∞

Gedruckt auf alterungsbeständigem, säurefreien Papier
Printed on acid-free paper

ISBN-10: 3-89821-907-0

ISBN-13: 978-3-89821-907-5

© *ibidem*-Verlag
Stuttgart 2008

Alle Rechte vorbehalten

Das Werk einschließlich aller seiner Teile ist urheberrechtlich geschützt. Jede Verwertung
außerhalb der engen Grenzen des Urheberrechtsgesetzes ist ohne Zustimmung des Verlages
unzulässig und strafbar. Dies gilt insbesondere für Vervielfältigungen,
Übersetzungen, Mikroverfilmungen und elektronische Speicherformen sowie die
Einspeicherung und Verarbeitung in elektronischen Systemen.

All rights reserved. No part of this publication may be reproduced, stored in or introduced into a retrieval
system, or transmitted, in any form, or by any means (electronical, mechanical, photocopying, recording or
otherwise) without the prior written permission of the publisher. Any person who does any unauthorized act
in relation to this publication may be liable to criminal prosecution and civil claims for damages.

Printed in Germany

*For My Fathers Halil İbrahim and Yusuf,
and My Island, My Son Ada*

CONTENTS

ACKNOWLEDGMENTS vii

INTRODUCTION 1

1. THE SKYSCRAPER 19

2. PSYCHOANALYTIC NEW YORK 46
    2.1. The Freudian Subject and the Built Environment 52
    2.2. The Lacanian Subject and the Built Environment 72

3. TOWER / POWER 92
    3.1. Foucault and the Panopticon 97
    3.2. Bourdieu and Symbolic Violence 108

4. SEPTEMBER 11 AND FALL OF THE TWIN TOWERS 116
    4.1. The Twin Towers 118
    4.2. The Politics of "Mourning and Melancholia"
        after September 11 122
    4.3. Rebuilding the Phallus: The Freedom Tower 127

CONCLUSION 134
BIBLIOGRAPHY 146

Acknowledgements

Many people contributed in various ways to the completion of this work, which was originally a Ph.D. dissertation. It gives me great pleasure to put in print my appreciation for Yusuf Eradam, my sublime supervisor at Ankara University, who, I know, has always been there for me. A very special thanks is due to Trevor Hope, who read the entire manuscript with meticulous attention and understood what I was trying to say more clearly than I did. He showed me so many directions to take I otherwise would not have seen. I also thank my professors on my dissertation board: Belgin Elbir, another heavenly figure in my life whose beautiful face and words I still have the chance to see and hear everyday, and Matthew Gumpert for their invaluable suggestions. I alone remain responsible for not being able to work out all their important suggestions. I am grateful to Christian Schön at *ibidem*-Verlag for making the process of revising and publishing this book feel so incredibly smooth.

A fellowship from The Turkish Fulbright Commission allowed me to begin work on this project, and to spend a year in New York, sitting and reading for endless hours at New York University's Bobst Library, ruthlessly overlooking Washington Square Park. I could not have asked for a more intellectually nourishing environment than NYU's American Studies Department. Faculty at NYU and fellow graduate students deeply influenced my idea of what American Studies is.

The very best thing about trying and trying to complete this work was that it gave me the chance to meet *the* city and its people: Cemal 'Ben' Demir, Mary Figueroa, Sam Sfez, Felix Rivera, Dominique Fowler, and Rodrigo Urbieta, who are in no way to be blamed for participating in my feats of procrastination. I also thank my dear friends Eylem Kiriş, Tuba Terci, Banu Ateş, Sırma Soran Gumpert, my sister Ezgi Kılıçer, and my mother Nuriye Kılıçer, who moved to another city to take care of my son while I was in New York, for helping me out when I most needed. The last but not the least, I thank my husband Alper Yarangümeli for always believing in me and supporting me in his own way.

My deepest heartfelt gratitude goes to my great island, my son Ada, who survived a year without his mother.

*[f]or here there is no place
that doesn't see you. You
must change your life.*

Rainer Maria Rilke "Archaic Torso of Apollo"

INTRODUCTION

This study of the American skyscraper offers a critical inspection of the ways in which "the center of the center," the vertical *temenos* of The United States, New York City is comprehended as *the* place for the American Dream of material success with its overwhelming bundle of skyscrapers. Theory used here explains the skyscraper phenomenon and provides a framework for understanding the circumstances and the people who created this phenomenon. The purpose of this study is to provide a socio-psychoanalytic lens through the works of psychoanalysts Sigmund Freud (1856-1939) and Jacques Lacan (1901-1981) together with social theorists Michel Foucault (1926-1984) and Pierre Bourdieu (1930-2002) in understanding why New York City has been expanding vertically and what this architectonic verticality tells us about the American. The study focuses on Manhattan because it is the very place where the skyscraper form was fully exploited. Manhattan also housed the "Twin Towers" of the World Trade Center before their fall in September 11, 2001.

The concept of architecture covers all types of construction: housing, temples, museums, skyscrapers and so on. In its more inclusive sense, an understanding and engagement with architecture is fundamental to any comprehensive understanding of culture. Buildings express the human capacity to organize and control the environment within which they live and thus to articulate their cultural world. Then one can argue that it is through architecture that particular cultures, also humanity, express and understand themselves and others. When one visits a foreign country, it is always either the natural environment; or the buildings, constructions that s/he first gets a glimpse of what that culture has produced. Take the Blue Mosque (Sultanahmet Camii) or Hagia Sophia (Aya Sofya; a church, a mosque, now a museum) out of Istanbul, you will not just lose two great architectural constructions, but the city itself. It is the buildings that make a city a city and it is through confrontation with the buildings of another culture that one can recognize both her/his and also their otherness.

Equally important is the fact that the built environment is the product of power relations within the community that created it: "Architecture is not the autonomous art it is often held out to be. Buildings are designed and constructed within a complex web of social and political concerns. To ignore the conditions under which architecture is practiced is to fail to understand the full social import of architecture" (Leach 14). Indeed it is often hard to find architectural texts that do not represent buildings as merely technical objects or art objects. Architectural discourse needs to see buildings in their social form, as social, political, and psychological objects in so far as they are invested with social meaning and shape social relations. Considering the fact that the skyscraper is mainly an American invention; the full social import of skyscrapers then will reflect social, political, and also symbolic and psychological concerns of Americans. Skyscrapers as architectural forms are the products of a way of seeing and envisioning the American way.

It is significant to acknowledge the fact that architecture reflects the mind of the society. Further, an individual's perception of buildings or the built environment is mediated through his/her consciousness. In attempting to expose the forces by which the built environment is generated and perceived, psychoanalysis provides a necessary lens to address the whole question of the social import that skyscrapers have and it becomes an indispensable tool in getting to understand a certain form of architecture and the mind frame of a society that invented it. Moreover, psychoanalysis deconstructs unconscious controlling mechanisms both in the human mind and in society. Accordingly, skyscrapers as modern images of towers function as a metaphor for social guardians, and in their essential phallomorphic form they stand as antitheses to the psychoanalytic metaphor that house is a womb, where all human beings belong. Moreover skyscrapers fuse the idea of power with masculinity in their essentially erect form. The effects of this type of architecturally symbolic guardianship go unnoticed for the most part. It is the main interest of this dissertation to unveil this dominance assisted through architecture, which is best exemplified in New York City, through a psychoanalytic lens engaged in a dialogue with Michel Foucault's rendering of the "panopticon" and Pierre Bourdieu's concept of "symbolic violence."

Architectural space is a medium through which to understand society. As German cultural theorist Siegfried Kracauer argues in "On Employment Agencies: The Construction of Space:" "Spatial images are the dreams of society. Wherever the hieroglyphics of any spatial image are deciphered, there the basis of social reality presents itself" (60). Obviously space is mediated by consciousness, and architecture is the product of a way of thinking. Space is never empty, as Foucault observes in "Of Other Spaces: Utopias and Heterotopias," it is always "saturated with qualities" (349).

Architecture, the art of creating spaces, develops hand in hand with powers of civilization. In building the first house people began to create, and equally important, began to control their own environment. In this light, architecture has arisen from the primitive hut in the humans' need and desire to have a say in their surroundings. Also in this way people have been able to communicate their needs and desires in their dwelling places and architectural products. Further, "the place" as one of the three common elements that every community has —others being the work and the people- leaves a significant mark in the history of their civilizations: "the characteristic buildings of each period are the memorials to their greatest institutions" (Mumford, 1934a 193). Each community then communicates its needs through the environment they built.

If architecture is a form of communication, then the city is a contingent web of discourses. Roland Barthes sees architecture as communication and in *The Pleasure of the Text* (1975) insists that "the city is a discourse and this discourse is truly a language" (92). Barthes' semiotic understanding of the city is one among hundreds of ways of looking at a city. Further, studying a city is a never-ending process; there is always more to learn and more to write. Indeed modern cities are as old as civilization itself, as the common root of the "city" and "civilization" in the Latin *civitas* implies (Kasinitz 8). When one attempts to study a "cosmetropolis" like New York City, the problem of the never-ending process comes with a deeper agony. Because the city is a system of representation, a complex cultural entity, with cities like New York complexity in the urban context reaches its zenith. "Cities are civilization and the study of cities involves the study of humankind. No one can master all there is to know about cities" (LeGates 18).

On the other hand, the embedded symbolism in urban context has proved to be a rich area of interest for scholars. Specifically Henri Lefebvre's *The Production of Space* (1974) was a groundbreaking text that established hitherto taken for granted links between the mental and physical spaces, including a range of spaces produced within a framework from the ideological, philosophical, and psychological aspects of spatial constructions to the "real" space that people inhabit in their everyday lives. Also Siegfried Giedion's *Space, Time and Architecture* (1967) offered an invaluable understanding for the vertical symbolism in the city. Kevin Lynch's *Image of the City* (1960), one of the earliest examples of study on urban imagery, for example, underlined the importance of the urban inhabitants' "ideas" for an understanding of the built environment.

On the literary side perhaps the most fruitful of renderings of the city came from the modernists who were both fascinated and repelled by the city. F. Scott Fitzgerald observes in *The Great Gatsby* (1926) when Nick and Gatsby are on their way to Manhattan:

> Over the great bridge, with sunlight through the girders making a constant flicker upon the moving cars, with the city rising up across the river in white heaps and sugar lumps all built with a wish out of nonolfactory money. The city seen from Queensboro Bridge is always the city seen for the first time, in its first wild promise of all the mystery and the beauty in the world (67).

It was this combination of mystery and promise of New York or precisely its very core Manhattan that enchanted the modernists. Fitzgerald writes in "My Lost City" (1936) that he knew "New York was home" in spite of "all that glamour and loneliness" (607-608). This ambivalent attitude towards the city is most explicit in John Dos Passos's *Manhattan Transfer* (1925). The fragmented narrative of *Manhattan Transfer* fuses the lost, but searching characters with skyscrapers towering necessarily above them transferring their perplexed emotions onto the built environment, specifically filling it with their lost ability to speak or even to think. The controlling metaphor of the oppressive towers of Manhattan makes the novel a perfect locus for the purposes of the study at hand.

Cities have always been an interest for scholars since the earliest times. There is a long tradition of writing about the cities, from Plato, who in *The Republic* wrote what an ideal polis should be like, to Aristotle, who in *The Politics* called man "zoon politikon" (the "political animal" or "the animal that belongs to a polis") to Shakespeare who wrote "the people are the city," (LeGates 22) to a twentieth century postmodern analysis of Bonaventure Hotel's lobby in Los Angeles by Fredric Jameson. Among archeologists, geographers, political scientists, economists, architects, urban planners, sociologists, literary writers, and other scholars, perhaps historians made the greatest contribution to understanding the evolution of cities.

Historians point that cities are as old as civilization itself. Humankind's rise to urban civilization took tens of thousands of years, but ever since the first true cities arose in Mesopotamia around 4000-3000 BCE, the influence of city-based cultures and the steady spread and increase of urban populations around the world have been the central facts of human history. The first stage of urban history is a shift from simple tribal communities and village-based agricultural production to the complex social, political, and economic systems exemplified by ancient cities like Ur and Babylon on the Euphrates. Further, in certain important respects, all the ancient cities are remarkably similar since most of them are walled (except in Egypt, where the surrounding desert may have been assumed to be a sufficient defense) and all contain a distinct stronghold area, separately walled, including a temple, a palace, and the central grain storage. Almost all of them were located along major rivers, and also, most of them featured some sort of pyramid or ziggurat (LeGates 21). New York, with its core borough Manhattan, then shares the qualities of an ancient city: Manhattan is built around Hudson River; it does not sport walls since it is an island where the surrounding ocean and rivers might be able to defend it; the cluster of downtown and midtown skyscrapers may function as the stronghold areas and each and every individual skyscraper is like a ziggurat totaling into one strong symbol in the skyline.

On the other hand, the cities of ancient Greece developed on a very different model probably because they were located on narrow mountain valleys rather than broad plains. The Greek city was small, economically self-sufficient and almost village-like in its social and political institutions. Greeks contributed to the evolution of the urban civilization with the concept of urban citizenship and democratic self-government, and at the core of this contribution was the concept of the "polis," which is sometimes translated as "city-state" and at other times is identified as the collective citizenry of a Greek city (LeGates 22). New York is also like a "city-state" in that it is economically more than self-sufficient, but in no way small.

Rome marks another sharp break in the history of urban life which began as a collection of villages in central Italy, emerged as a powerful republic similar to the earlier Greek cities but then exploded into a giant metropolis and a city of world empire that extended from Persia to the borders of Scotland. With the expansion of the empire, Roman literature, philosophy, and art were also spread establishing the basis for a widespread cultural dominance. Unlike the Greek polis, in Rome a citizenship of imperial privilege established a strict hierarchy of patricians, clients, and plebeians. However, Rome's contributions to civilization like its roads, elevated water pipes and sewers set new standards (LeGates 22). Rome's symbolic name "Babylon the Great" stands both as an antithesis to the Heavenly Jerusalem and as *the city* on earth. New York, too, is *the* city in its glamorous chaos.

In the early Middle Ages most of Europe went back to rural conditions, and serfdom became widespread under a system of warlord feudalism, because of the raids by Vikings from the North and invasion by North African Arabs on the South. During this period cities of Islam like Samara and Baghdad were the real centers of power that surpassed European cities in wealth and power. But the conditions changed in the late middle ages, and cities became true centers of commerce, culture, and community again with great trading towns that inevitably gave way to their growing power and political independence.

The defensive walls of medieval cities clearly separated the urban where industry and commerce led the life and the rural where agricultural pursuits gave shape to living conditions. Within the town walls economic and social life were organized by guilds, while the church was responsible for taking care of citizens' spiritual needs and established a framework for social ritual and communal unity. What characterized medieval cities were the cathedrals, guildhouses, charitable institutions, universities, and marketplaces (LeGates 22-23). What characterizes New York City is its skyscrapers that have dwarfed the cathedrals.

In Europe the slow decay of medieval urban unity began with the Renaissance and the rise of monarchies. The new national rulers built their royal palaces outside the traditional urban centers, like Louis XIV's Versailles. They intervened into the existing urban fabric by building large boulevards and squares which they saw fit for the display of power. The Enlightenment and the Age of Revolutions shattered the divine right of kings and reestablished the political power of the urban commercial interests. The capitalist city of the Industrial Revolution created an entirely new urban condition and established the physical, social, economic, and political preconditions of all that was to come after. The modern city emerges with the Industrial Revolution. Modern capitalist city also created a social hierarchy -like that of the Romans- between the property-owning bourgeoisie and the proletariat who had no property to own. Middle-class employed strategies to protect themselves from the poverty of the proletariat and fled to the suburbs. Suburbanization resulted in segregation by social class and it is still one of the features of the modern city. Especially after World War II, with the popular usage of the automobile suburbs became more like segregated sanctuaries of class privilege. Suburbanization reaches its heights in Los Angeles where all the existing rules and natural boundaries of urban development break. Sometimes dismissed as a mere network of suburbs in search of a city, Los Angeles emerges as a city not with a single downtown but multiple "downtowns" heavily relying on automobile, a radically decentralized urban paradigm poised on the edge of postmodernity (LeGates 23-24).

The historical overview of the city, though roughly given, shows that the physical organization of the city has tremendous effects on its citizens, since "how a city looks and how its spaces are organized forms a material base upon which a range of possible sensations and social practices can be thought about, evaluated, and achieved" (Harvey 67). However, how physical environment shapes and is shaped by social life is still a big question.

One architectural historian, one of the greatest public intellectuals of the twentieth century America, Lewis Mumford, like Shakespeare, always kept the human dimension of cities in his works. His masterpiece *The City in History* (1961) and an earlier rendering of the same topic *The Culture of Cities* (1938) have left an inerasable mark on future urban planners.

For Mumford cities are expressions of the human spirit and cities exist to contribute to the ever-evolving human personality. He forwards his main propositions about city planning, and the individual and social human potential of urban life in "What is a City?" (1937). The central question for Mumford in the essay is: "what is the city as a social institution?" (93). He then goes on to lay out the sociological concept of the city around two primary groups which are common to all communities: the family and the neighborhood which are "all housed in permanent structures, within a relatively limited area" (93). The permanent structures are ever changing buildings and clusters of buildings that "house" communities together. For Mumford the city in its complete sense is "a geographic plexus, an economic organization, an institutional process, *a theater of social action*, and an aesthetic symbol of collective unity" (1937 94) [emphasis mine].

Mumford takes "the social drama" as the core ingredient of the city, and this proved to be a topic that he returned again and again: "The city fosters art and is art; the city creates theater, that man's more purposive activities are focused, and work out, through conflicting and cooperating personalities, events, groups, into more significant culminations" (1937 94). Significantly, the built environment, or physical organization of the city has the power to "deflate" or "frustrate" this collective drama (94). For example, Mumford criticizes the new plan for Bryant Park in downtown Manhattan in his "Modern Design and The New Bryant Park" (1934) because it does not "encourage circulation," hence frustrating the collective drama: "The worst [weakness] probably is the fact that the park is planned on a false axis, with a grand entrance up a flight of steps from Sixth Avenue, and with a fountain on the terrace. [...] The plan does not encourage circulation" (123).

Mumford believed that the skyscraper period was coming to an end, and it had reached the peak of its development. His never changing humanist attitude holds true for his proposal instead of skyscrapers to begin all over again on a new line, which means:

> [p]lanning long, shallow buildings—under ten stories— in multiple rows; eliminating the partly unused and therefore extravagant express elevator shafts; providing daylight and natural ventilation for every worker and as much direct sunlight as is tolerable; turning roofs into noon-hour recreation spaces and providing for pedestrian movement and for shops at the street level on the inner sides of the buildings (1933 101).

Jane Jacobs, too, echoes Mumford's notion of the "social drama" in her notion of the "street ballet" in her groundbreaking *The Death and Life of Great American Cities* (1961) which she dedicated to New York City. Until her death in 2006, Jacobs fiercely fought for her and others' right to "ballet on the street." To her, life in the neighborhood, on the sidewalk was essentially a ballet that engenders urban vitality, which in turn comes from residents' participation in an urban human activity (Jacobs, 1961 50-54). Although she derided Mumford's *The Culture of Cities* as "largely a morbid and biased catalog of ills" (1961 20), she shared with Mumford a great love for New York. As self-taught New Yorkers, Jacobs and Mumford did not receive any professional training in urban planning or architecture, yet they looked for ways to increase human contact in the city. Called by *The New York Times Book Review* "perhaps the most influential single work in the history of town planning" *The Death and Life of Great American Cities* is like a love song written to Hudson Street, where Jacobs lived, and its residents in Greenwich Village. In the book Jacobs lays out her basic notions of what makes a city livable and her desire for contact in a community, attacking "the principles and aims that have shaped modern, orthodox city planning and rebuilding" (4).

Mumford's and Jacobs's keen interest in the spatial organization of the city comes from the very fact that cities among anything else are physical artifacts made by people. And the ways in which people make these artifacts show how they envision a future for themselves, how they envision themselves. Exemplified in William Cooper's 1783 couplet, "God made the Country, Man Made the Town" (Kasinitz 3), the dichotomy between nature and the man-made city, also points to another dichotomy between "God the Creator" and human beings as creators. As Raymond Williams writes in his *The Country and the City* (1973):

> On the country has gathered the idea of a natural way of life: of peace, innocence, and simple virtue. On the city has gathered the idea of an achieved center: of learning, communication, light. Powerful hostile associations have also developed: on the city as a place of noise, worldliness and ambition; on the country as a place of backwardness, ignorance, limitation (1).

It is in this dichotomy between the urban and rural areas that the evolution of the big city, the metropolis, took the sides further away. Especially with New York, with its "determination to remove its territory as far from the natural as humanly possible" (11) as Dutch architect Rem Koolhaas points in his *Delirious New York: A Retroactive Manifesto for Manhattan* (1978), the separation becomes grand. French architect and urban theorist Le Corbusier (Charles Edouard Jeanneret) sees Manhattan as "inhuman" too. In his article "The Fairy Catastrophe" from the 1936 book *When the Cathedrals Were White*, he calls New York City "a catastrophe" but "it is a beautiful catastrophe" (617) devised by humans.

Indeed, New York is one of the most elaborate artifacts of the human imagination. Today, it is one of the greatest cultural and financial centers of the world, which is known for its alluring beauty and its influence. Although for many people the history of New York begins in 1524 when Giovanni da Verrazano, an Italian working for France, entered today's New York Harbor, New York is yet *the oldest* major city in the United States with its eleven-thousand-year of human history that began through the end of the Ice Ages, when the first pioneering "Indians" arrived (Cantwell and Wall 3-4). It is maybe because New York looks larger than life with its immense collection of skyscrapers turning their faces into the future that eleven-thousand-year of human history sounds like an oxymoron. As the most important element of New York's built environment, the skyscrapers with their ambitious thrust into the heavens give a feeling of fantasy that one is accustomed to see on the screen. Film-makers, writers, and everyone who had been exposed to New York through mediated or unmediated ways cannot escape its profound influence.

But what is it that makes New York so special, so different from other places? Editors of *Empire City: New York Through the Centuries* (2002) Kenneth T. Jackson and David S. Dunbar list ten significant factors:

1) Tempo. New Yorkers walk faster, work longer, eat later, and compete harder than most Americans do. If you can "talk that talk and walk that walk" you are a New Yorker.

2) Diversity. New York has always been multicultural, multiracial, multireligious, and multilingual. As early as the 1640s eighteen different languages were already being spoken in New Amsterdam. In 1880 it had the world's largest immigrant labor force; it still does. In 1999, more than eleven of every twenty New Yorkers are immigrants or the children of immigrants, and the metropolitan region has more Jews than Tel Aviv, more Italians than Florence, more Dominicans than Santo Domingo, and more Irish than Dublin.

3) Tolerance. Diversity has led to a reluctant acceptance of difference. The city's circumstances force residents to control and even to repress their prejudices. The standard was set four hundred years ago by the Dutch. In the early seventeenth century, when Puritan Boston was banishing Anne Hutchinson from the city because of doctrinal disagreements, the West India Company, out of commercial worries that bigotry might threaten trade and discourage immigration was welcoming all.

4) Density. Relative to other American cities, New York has been overcrowded ever since the Dutch settlers came together below Wall Street for protection. Many flooded the city, as many fled from it, but there have always been others ready to take their place.

5) Orientation toward public transportation. A century ago, the United States had the best and most extensive public transportation in the world, but since that time Americans built superhighways and became dependent on automobiles. But not New Yorkers.

6) Domination of the central business district primacy. Since 1945, the vitality of big cities shifted to suburbs, and once bustling department stores, the signatures of cities are only memories now. Not in New York. Macy's is still "the world's largest" department store. New York did not lose its city center and downtown.

7) Keeping a substantial middle and upper class. North American residential pattern is for the rich to live in the suburbs and the poor to live in the middle. New York is no exception, but still, though comparatively, the middle class has not abandoned New York. Nor did the upper class; Manhattan is the richest county in the nation on a per capita basis, the wealthiest zip code in America is 10021, and the highest real estate values in the country are along Fifth Avenue, Park Avenue, and Central Park West.

8) Environmental sustenance. New Yorkers' energy consumption is low by American standards because of their reliance on public transportation, and because of the fact that many of them live in apartments which use fewer fossil fuels to be heated and to be cooled.

9) Success in public housing. In 1937 United States Housing Act made it possible for the federal government to build decent, low-cost houses, the so-called "projects" for the needy. By the end of 1962 more than two million people were living in the projects. But in 2002 the projects are considered a failure because many of them are crime ridden. As a result, cities across the

nation tore down the complexes. Not New York. Still thousands of families are on the waiting list, and the projects themselves are in remarkably good shape.

10) Safe environment. In contrast to the city's notorious image fed by movies and television, New York has never statistically been among the nation's most dangerous cities. Homicide rate in the city is so low that New York is not even in the top hundred most violent American cities. Also automobile fatality rate is low because New Yorkers walk or take the train to many destinations. In other words, New York is safe because of its density and its subways, not in spite of them (1-6).

These elements have placed New York to a unique position, contributing to its almost mythical existence in people's minds.

As William Dean Howells writes in *A Hazard of New Fortunes* (1889), New York is the only city that belongs to the entire country (153). In the course of the nineteenth century New York's centrality was reflected in the symbolically identifying points in its landscape: Wall Street supplied the country with capital; Ellis Island channeled its labor; Fifth Avenue set its social trends; Madison Avenue advertised its products; Broadway entertained it. Further, it was the nation's major source for news and opinion; it attracted those seeking cosmopolitan freedom; and as the biggest city of the biggest state it exercised extraordinary influence in national politics (Burrows and Wallace 18). Nothing much changed since then.

New York had also served as the seat of the national government for a brief time between 1785 and 1790. Though no longer the capital by law it remained as the spiritual capital of the United States. During the Cold War, New York and the country's de jure capital Washington emerged as partners: "the city on the Hudson the multinational empire's commercial center, the city on the Potomac its military core" (Burrows and Wallace 19). But again, New York is also a city that belongs to "the entire world," with its population of immigrants from all over the world, and as the seat of the United Nations. Underlying the point the veteran *New Yorker* essayist E. B. White, in his wonderfully poetic rendering of New York City, *Here is New York* (1949), writes:

> Along the East River, from the razed slaughterhouses of Turtle Bay [...] men are carving out the permanent headquarters of the United Nations—the greatest housing projects of them all. In its stride, New York takes on one more interior city, to shelter, this time, all governments, and to clear the slum called war. New York is not a capital city—it is not a national capital or a state capital. But it is by way of becoming the capital of the world (54-55).

Walt Whitman, the poet laureate of New York City, was perhaps the first poet to capture the spirit of his great city. He calls New York "the great place of the Western continent, the heart, the rain, the focus, the main spring, the pinnacle, the extremity, the no more beyond of the western world" (Jackson and Dunbar 247). Whitman's poetry essentially expresses the energy and diversity of New York City that was to become the capital of the modern world. He writes in "Manhatta" (1860): "I see that the word of my city is that word from of old, / Because I see that word nested in nests of water-bays, superb, / Rich, hemm'd thick all around with sailships, an island / sixteen miles long, solid-founded, / Numberless crowded streets, high growths of iron, slender, strong, light, / splendidly uprising toward clear skies, / ... / City of hurried and sparkling waters! city of spires and masts! / City nested in bays! my city! (253) The name Manhattan is derived from an Algonquian term "Manhatta" meaning "island of hills" foreshadowing what was to become an island of manmade hills of skyscrapers and it is this "aboriginal name" that comes to Whitman essentially as vertical in shape and that shares with him the energy of being one big whole with the past of the city. In the nineteenth century and today, New York has been a city of extremes and excess that looked skyward. Historian Edward Spann clarifies the point:

> Although it included a wide range of human existence, New York was best known in its extremes, as a city capable of shedding the most brilliant light and casting the deepest shadows. Perhaps no place in the world evoked such extremes of love and hate, often in the same person. In its slums, dirt, materialism, violence, congestion, rush, politics and

municipal mismanagement, it could depress, degrade and offend, the human spirit. In its wealth, intelligence, power, opportunities, and in the seemingly endless wonders of its streets, it could exalt, exhilarate and, occasionally, even charm strangers and citizens alike. The new metropolis was radically imperfect, but its imperfections were those of a masterwork of collective human spirit and masterful presence in the world (426).

Before Whitman though, Washington Irving was at pains to "create" a myth for New York City. In *Knickerbocker's History of New York* (1809) Irving set out to portray his native city as "having an antiquity thus extending back into the regions of doubt and fable" (7) without ever knowing that his beloved "Gotham" had an eleven-thousand-year of human history. Irving's *History of New York* is a mock-epic, a collection of fact and fiction that consciously plays with myth and history, with its narrow minded and showy narrator Diedrich Knickerbocker who is jealous of his predecessors "Dan Homer and Dan Virgil" for being able to summon up "waggish deities" to descend to earth and "play their pranks, upon its wondering inhabitants" (Burrows and Wallace 12). Knickerbocker thinks that the new world lacks the mythic past and its imaginative charms that Homer and Virgil made use of so well, so he invents one.

Irving had begun his efforts at devising a line of descent for New York in the *Salmagundi* papers (1807) in which he gave the name "Gotham" to his city: "Repeatedly *Salmagundi* referred to Manhattan as the 'antient city of Gotham,' or 'the wonder loving city of Gotham.' In the context of the pieces—mocking commentaries on the mores of fashionable New Yorkers—the well-known name of Gotham served to underscore their depiction of Manhattan as a city of self-important and foolish people" (Burrows 12). Gotham is a real village in Nottinghamshire, England, and its inhabitants are known for their follies told in jokes (like the Turkish Laz jokes) or "merry tales" since the twelfth century. But Gothamites are not mere fools; they are wise enough to play fools. Since Irving New York's nickname is Gotham.

Edwin G. Burrows and Mike Wallace, the editors of by far the best narrative history written on New York City, *Gotham: A History of New York City to 1898* (1999), write that although Irving's creation story never passed into popular lore, a simpler version did, that the Dutch bought Manhattan from the natives for twenty-four dollars. This myth too, like Irving's, is centered around the notion of New York as a city of tricksters: "What gives the story its legendary quality is the host of meanings attached to the event, starting with the notion—smuggled in via the word 'purchased'—that the 'Island Manhattes' was a piece of property that could be owned and transferred" (14). What is more important, this tale is always recounted with a malicious satisfaction; tellers are tickled by their understanding that the Dutch tricked the Indians with only twenty-four dollars (or a handful of beads, buttons, and other trinkets in some versions) into handing over what became the most valuable piece of land in the world. Racial patronage is clear in this, with primitive savages dazzled by the cheap showy trinkets of civilization. But more telling is that the people who made the agreement with the Dutch did not live in Manhattan, therefore did not have any property rights to "sell" the island, as it appears from a later repurchase agreement (Burrows and Wallace 14-15). After all, maybe it was the "civilized" Europeans who got tricked.

Further, Burrows and Wallace point out that this purchase story lays a "genetic" foundation of deal driving, sharp practice, moneymaking, and real estate in New Yorkers. Also "it proclaims a city whose acquisition was based not on conquest but on contract," and the notion that New York is rooted in a commercial transaction suggests New York would become a city of deal makers, a city of commerce, a City of Capital:

> New York would not become a warrior city, living by raids on its hinterland. Even when centuries later it emerged as an imperial center, it was never a military stronghold. [...] Nor would New York become an urban theocracy, a citadel of priests. No shrines or temples were erected to which swarms of pilgrims flocked to pay religious tribute or receive inspiration. Despite the formidable number of churches established here, Mammon ruled, not God. Nor would New York become a great governmental hub, with grand baroque avenues radiating out from imposing seats of state power. There was no regal court to dis-

pense largesse to all comers or lure peasants to bask in its splendors. No monarch founded seats of learning so preeminent as to attract truth-seekers from the ends of the earth. Its civic chieftains would be merchants, bankers, landlords, lawyers; its mightiest buildings, office towers (Burrows and Wallace 15-16).

Indeed "Mammon" rules in New York as Ambrose Bierce ironically gives the gist in his *The Devil's Dictionary* (1906) with the entry "Mammon": "The god of the world's leading religion. His chief temple is the holy city of New York" (85). In the New Testament Mammon is a personification of wealth and greed as an evil spirit. In New York (and else where) people worship money in churches disguised as skyscrapers that reach onto heavens.

Burrows and Wallace chart the ways New York's development has been crucially shaped by its shifting position in an evolving economy: From its beginnings as a constellation of Indian communities encamped around the mouth of the Hudson River, the area was pulled into the imperial world system Europeans had begun fashioning after Columbus's voyages. Founded in 1624 as a *trading* post on the periphery of a Dutch mercantile empire, New Amsterdam lay at the outermost edge of a new born web of international relationships. It remained a relatively insignificant backwater, to which its Dutch masters paid minimal attention, as they had far greater interest in harvesting the profits available in Asia (spices), Africa (slaves), and South America (sugar). However, once forcibly appended to the rising British Empire in 1664 New York assumed a more prominent role. Charles II granted his brother the Duke of York (later James II) a large area including Manhattan. The British seized the city in the same year and the settlement was renamed New York in honor of the duke. It became a vital seaport supplying agricultural products to England's star colonies (the Caribbean sugar islands) while also serving the English as a strategic base for hemispheric military operations against the French, the latest entrants in the imperial race for dominance. After the American Revolution, New York emerged as the young nation's premier linkage point between industrializing Europe and its North American agricultural hinterland. The city skillfully positioned itself with respect to three of the most dynamic regions of the nineteenth century global economy—England's manufacturing midlands, the cotton producing slave South, and the agricultural Midwest—and it prospered by shipping cotton and wheat east while transferring labor, capital, manufactured and cultural goods west. After the Civil War, the metropolis became the principal facilitator of America's own industrialization and imperial westward expansion. Capital flowed through and from its great banks and stock exchanges to western rails, mines, land, and factories; it became the major portal for immigrant workers; and it exported the country's industrial and agricultural commodities. By the end of the nineteenth century New York gained the ability to direct, not just channel America's industrialization. Financiers like J. P. Morgan established nationwide corporations and housed them in the city, making Manhattan the country's corporate headquarters. When World War I ended European dominance, and the United States became a creditor nation, New York began to compete with London as the focus of global economy. It finally captured that position after World War II when the United States emerged as a superpower. In the following decades, when American corporations and banks expanded overseas, New York became headquarters for the new multinational economy; and the arrival of the United Nations made New York a global political capital as well as a financial one. However, New York was more than simply a point of merger; it was a place of ever increasing potency in global affairs, and as the United States evolved from colony to empire, the city migrated from the edge to the center of the world (15-19).

New York's rise to dominance in the world is inscribed in its skyline. As the city's economy moved from commercial to industrial to corporate only the styles of its piercing skyscrapers changed. New York kept its towers in an unashamed display of economic power, function, and poetic creativity, serving a strong symbolism. As German philosopher Theodor Adorno argues in "Functionalism Today", even the functional may attract the symbolic. Symbols are born out of the need to identify with one's surroundings, and humans attach symbolic significance to even technical objects like the skyscraper. The following chapter is a research into the "beginnings" of the skyscraper form, and its attendant function and symbolism.

1. THE SKYSCRAPER

> Skyscrapers [r]epresent a building type which with wonderful exactness reflects the civilization that produced them. They are not only America's most characteristic representative in the domain of architecture, they are also miniatures of America itself. Whoever studies the skyscraper, studies America.
>
> Thomas A. P. van Leeuwen, *The Skyward Trend of Thought: The Metaphysics of the American Skyscraper*, 1988.

Since its invention at the turn of the nineteenth century, the skyscraper has always been a powerful symbol for America. Since then the skyscrapers have dominated the skyline of the largest cities both in the United States and in the world. But New York differs from other places in the number, size, and typicality of its skyscrapers. Chicago may have been the place of birth for the skyscraper, but Manhattan became its home, and a century ago it was already assuming the towerlike form that has distinguished it ever since. The Singer, Met Life, Woolworth, Chrysler, and Empire State were successively the tallest buildings in the world, as was the World Trade Center. By 1974, New York contained as many tall buildings of sixty or more stories as all other cities combined (Jackson and Dunbar 3), and even today the skyline of Manhattan is impossible to confuse with any other.

The soaring, powerful symbol functions in two opposing directions: while objectifying the fears of the new technology, it at the same time objectifies the hopes for the same technology that it would further the living conditions of city dwellers. In the nineteenth century the skyscraper was perceived as a newly invented urban landmark that reflected the urban culture of the time, it also helped shape that culture. Significantly Le Corbusier's oxymoron for Manhattan that it is "a beautiful, fairy catastrophe" is "the lever of hope" for him, because the neoclassical architecture of the previous century, in its imitation of the earlier styles "covered the earth with ugly and soulless works.

Bestiality of money. The twentieth century aspires to grace, suppleness" (618). It is in New York that grace and suppleness will be achieved, because for Le Corbusier New York is the place for the new metropolis: "It gushes up. I cannot forget New York, Vertical city, now that I have had the happiness of seeing it, raised in the sky. It is the first place in the world on the scale of new times, the work yard of our era" (1936 611). However, according to Le Corbusier, because skyscrapers in New York are not an element in city planning, but a "banner in the sky," and further they "are too small and there are too many of them," they create "a complete urban disaster" (1936 614-615).

Today all the metropolises around the world have their *prestigious* skyscrapers and the race to build the highest skyscraper still goes on. As of 2006 the highest skyscraper in the world is "Taipei 101" of Taiwan completed in 2004, towering up to 1667 feet with 101 stories. However there are proposals for the superlative race that will surpass "Taipei 101" like the "Freedom Tower" of New York City, which is going to be built to stand erect in a symbolic 1,776 feet in the area where once stood the "Twin Towers" of World Trade Center before the attacks of September 11, 2001; furthermore "Burj Dubai" of United Arab Emirates is under construction to reach to an amazing 2,666 feet with 160 stories, to be completed around 2008. Ironically both will be built by the acclaimed American architecture company Skidmore, Owings & Merrill.

Manhattan has fabulously solid bedrock, called the Manhattan schist, which makes the island such a congenial place for the building of skyscrapers (Glanz and Lipton 16). The study contends that the decisions for constructing skyscrapers in Manhattan were based on contingent needs and desires: the needs were imposed by the fact that Manhattan was an island with limited space (land economics) and a soaring population; the desires were motivated by notions of corporate imagery and power. The massive energy of late nineteenth century commercialism found its cathartic venue in the skyscraper. Equally important is the related consequence of the rise in land values which made the skyscraper desirable in economic terms and the competitive economy made it a success. Therefore, skyscrapers fulfilled both symbolic and functional ends.

Most of the studies on the skyscraper form have been conducted by chiefly architectural historians and critics. These studies can be roughly divided into two: 1) what is a skyscraper and what are the criteria for defining it, and 2) what is or should be the style in building the skyscraper. Few exceptions aside, they seem not to be interested in an understanding of social and psychological context. This study aims to fill in that gap.

A great majority of scholars associate the skyscraper form with the idea of modernity not only because of their almost simultaneous dominance in rendering the urban environment, but because what they *tell* about people who are exposed to their influences. For example, urban sociologist Marshall Berman writes in his classic 1982 critique of modernism *All That is Solid Melts into Air*:

> There is a mode of vital experience – experience of space and time, of the self and others, of life's possibilities and perils – that is shared by men and women all over the world today. I will call this body of experience 'modernity.' To be modern is to find ourselves in an environment that promises adventure, power, joy, growth, transformation of ourselves and the world – and, at the same time, that threatens to destroy everything we are. Modern environments and experiences cut across all boundaries of geography and ethnicity, of class and nationality, of religion and ideology; in this sense, modernity can be said to unite all mankind. But it is a paradoxical unity, a unity of disunity; it pours us all into a maelstrom of perpetual disintegration and renewal, of struggle and contradiction, of ambiguity and anguish. To be modern is to be part of a universe in which, as Marx said, 'all that is solid melts into air' (15).

Modern life, as portrayed by Berman and modernist writers, is characterized by an overwhelming sense of transitoriness, fragmentation, and change[1].

---

[1] Berman's quote from Karl Marx and Friedrich Engels' *The Communist Manifesto* (1848) is part of the theorists' critique of the bourgeois epoch, with "constant revolutionizing of production, uninterrupted disturbance of all social conditions, everlasting uncertainty and agitation" (223) is different from earlier epochs. The only way for the bourgeoisie to exist is to revolutionize the instruments and relations of production and through these the whole relations of society: "All fixed, fast-frozen relations, with their train of ancient and

That everything is pregnant with its anti-thesis gives the idea of change its ambivalence, and thereby the equally ambivalent reactions to it. It is this very feeling when Hamlet almost cries his heart out, saying "the world is out of joint" or when Yeats writes in "The Second Coming" that "the centre cannot hold".

Further, the experience of time and space is doomed to be chaotic because change and transformation leave no ground for a secured center: "[t]here is abundant evidence to suggest that most 'modern' writers have recognized that the only secure thing about modernity is its insecurity, its penchant, even, for 'totalizing chaos'" (Harvey 11). Because of the ephemerality of things, especially of time and space, makes any sense of historical continuity difficult to preserve, the modernist time is one that of rupture.

Accordingly the great modernist T. S. Eliot begins his seminal essay "Tradition and the Individual Talent" (1919) as follows: "In English writing we seldom speak of tradition, though we occasionally apply its name in deploring its absence" (1092). Eliot's assertion is essentially about continuity and rupture: tradition signifying continuity of established forms, individual talent signifying a rupture from these established forms. However, what is significant for Eliot in achieving a higher form of art is the understanding that "[t]he past should be altered by the present as much as the present is directed by the past" (1093); in other words, the poet both belongs to the tradition "of the dead," and he, simultaneously, through his innovative style, makes it: he shapes it and is shaped by it. Thus rupture or novelty emerges by way of being engulfed in tradition. With Eliot, the poet challenges and revises the tradition to which he yields: "What happens when a new work of art is created," Eliot stresses, "is something that happens simultaneously to all the works of art that preceded it" (1090, 1093). Surely for Eliot tradition does not mean some unchanging and determined pattern but rather a kind of resource to be reworked through the powers of the individual artist.

---

venerable prejudices and opinions are swept away, all new-formed ones become antiquated before they can ossify. All that is solid melts into air, all that is holy is profaned" (Marx and Engels 223).

The same holds true for the architectural art where the skyscrapers form the latest chain and at the same time enforcing a kind of rupture in an architectural tradition of building towers. This is why this study contends that the skyscraper is "mainly" an American invention. But what is a skyscraper? What makes one tall building just a tall building and the other a skyscraper?

Although in popular usage the word "skyscraper" means a tall building, architectural historians have debated over the exact nature of the elements that constitute a "true" skyscraper. Tall buildings made their general appearance some years before the word was used to describe them. Before its invention, before the late nineteenth century, skyscraper as a word was used not for tall buildings. The 1933 edition of the *Oxford English Dictionary* cites six definitions of the word: a triangular sky sky-sail; a high-standing horse; a bicycle with a very high wheel in the back; an exceptionally tall man; an exaggerated tale, a tall tale, and finally "a high building of many stories, especially one of those characteristic of American cities." However the 1963 edition of the same dictionary cites only the last definition with an important omission: "a very tall building" (Bletter 110). The change in definition of the same word refers to a fact in the evolution of the skyscraper, it maintains its height but now it is not localized to American cities, it is everywhere.

Architectural historians agree that the skyscraper was invented in the United States, but there are debates over the birthplace of the skyscraper: Is it Chicago or New York City? Many of the earlier histories of the skyscraper –like Carl W. Condit's- refer to William Le Baron Jenney's Home Life Insurance Company Building in Chicago built in 1884-1855 as the first skyscraper. Condit in his *The Rise of the Skyscraper* (1952), which is probably the best-known history of the skyscraper, refers to Jenney's building as "the first building of framed or skeletal construction and hence the first true skyscraper" (28). Col. W. A. Starrett, too, refers to the building as "the first of all skyscrapers" (237). Starrett also considers Jenney as the inventor of the skyscraper because of his use of steel frame. However others, like Winston Weisman's "A New View of Skyscraper History" (1970), refer to Equitable Life Insurance Company Building in New York built in 1868-1870 as the first skyscraper. Weisman says that Equitable Life Insurance Company Building was twice taller than the average

23

office buildings in its day and it comprised of "the necessary ingredients of the early skyscraper": height, elevator, and iron construction (Bletter 114).

There are various opinions on the criteria that would distinguish a skyscraper from a tall building. These opinions take the technological process (use of the steel-frame etc.) or architectural form as bases. Generally, a building can be determined by what function it serves but the skyscraper is distinguished from others by its dimensions. Although the first skyscrapers were mostly office buildings, not all office buildings were skyscrapers. So if a building is a residential space or a commercial space does not have any relevance to determining its type as a skyscraper. Whether a museum is small or large, there is never any doubt what building type it represents. Therefore the question of function does not serve the distinction (Bletter 110-111).

The image of the skyscraper requires a vertical, towerlike form. But tallness depends on urban context which is ever-shifting: the eye can distinguish a tall building according to its surrounding buildings and when a taller building is constructed, the one that was tall before becomes instantly dwarfed. Then tallness is not enough only, one needs a context. It needs to be a distinctive landmark.

Architectural historian J. Carson Webster in his essay entitled "The Skyscraper: Logical and Historical Considerations" (1959) studies the form comprehensively, including its technological, economic, psychological, and aesthetic functions:

1. Essential characteristics (the end).
    a) Great height (relative to buildings).
    b) Arrangement (interior) in stories.
    c) Utmost space and light (potentially) in each story.

2. Necessary means.
    a) A structural system adequate to achieving the essential characteristics taken together. To date this means skeleton construction. [This must be amended to include flat-slab and box fram-

ing, which are not framing systems in the strict sense of serial column-and-beam construction.]²

b) Materials necessary to the structural system, above all steel (iron and reinforced concrete as possible alternatives), and fireproofing, heat-resisting material.

c) Passenger elevators.

3. Favoring conditions.

a) Economic –such as high value of land; availability of labor and capital; etc.

b) Social –such as living in large groups; enterprise; organization of work; publicity; etc.

c) Technological –such as availability of suitable tools, processes and sources of power; development of plumbing, heating, etc.; growth of engineering; development of the craft of building to a certain point, etc.

d) Psychological –desires (conscious or unconscious) which a tall form can express.

e) Aesthetic –liking for height; preference for the effect of towers related to lower buildings; etc (127).

Unlike many others who see the steel frame, or the previous iron cast frame as a prerequisite for the skyscraper, Webster does not take it as an absolute, but all the same he maintains that it is simply the most effective way to achieve great height (Bletter 112). Webster also places the first skyscraper in Chicago. Likewise Lewis Mumford, "the prince" of America's architecture critics, in his *The Brown Decades: A Study of the Arts in America 1865-1895* (1959), puts height and steel frame into a broader context that the question of the first skyscraper becomes not that important:

> The priority for the invention of steel frame or skeleton construction has been disputed; it was claimed by, among others, L. H. Buffington, Minnesota architect, who applied for a patent; but the whole question becomes a little absurd when one remembers that the traditional American frame house is based on an exactly comparable method of

---

² Addendum in original.

construction. The new elements were the fireproofing of the component materials, and the more exact calculations made possible through the use of steel, along with the opportunity of increasing the height of the structure, which was limited only by the strength of the foundations and the expense of vertical transportation (138).

The disagreement between the pro-Chicago (Condit and Webster) and pro-New York (Weisman) architectural historians concerning the first skyscraper has not been solved. But whether it is Chicago or New York is not important in terms of the study at hand since the impulse to build tall and the subsequent evolution of the skyscraper form is most evident and most well-known in New York City.

Although architectural discourse has traditionally represented buildings as art objects or technical objects, buildings are also social objects in that they are invested with social meaning and shape social relations. Especially with grand buildings like skyscrapers which occupy a large space both on the land and in the air –not to mention the imaginary space in the mind of the observer- the problem of the built form exerting social influences becomes more important. For example, The Regional Plan Commission of New York in its studies on the planning of Manhattan entitled "The Regional Survey and Plan" (1931) asks but does not answer a crucial question on the social aspect of the skyscraper:

> All accept the skyscraper as something which serves human needs, but judge it differently as to the value of this service. All know that it has become the dominant feature in the structural composition of large American cities. But is it also to be the dominant feature in the social organization of all urban life in America? [...] If we attempt to answer this question we would have had to go deeper than we have dared to go in the Regional Survey and Plan" (Adams et al. 99-117).

Everything may be questioned within the framework of the Regional Plan, except the skyscraper: "We will have to accept the skyscraper as inevitable and proceed to consider how it can be made healthy and beautiful" (Adams et al. 114). However, Lewis Mumford does not take the skyscraper form for granted and he analyzes the skyscraper in social terms in *The Brown Decades*, where he famously concluded:

> Socially the skyscraper gave encouragement to all our characteristic American weaknesses: our love of abstract magnitude, our interest in land-gambling, our desire for conspicuous waste; it did this to such an extent that it is almost heresy to call attention to the defects of the tall building: the dubious economy of vertical transportation at the magnificent maximum rate of nine mile per hour: the waste of cubbage in the unused sections of express elevator shafts –to say nothing of the shutting out of sunlight and air, and the intensification of congestion on the streets and in the subways (139). [emphasis mine]

Mumford's stand about the "characteristic American weaknesses" and especially American's "love for abstract magnitude" is important. This interest in size makes itself clear both in largeness and smallness. On the large part the most obvious examples come from the architecture of skyscrapers of course, from large portions of food served in American restaurants and from large American cars; on the small part most of the examples come from technological products such as cell phones, mp3 players, computers and the like, becoming smaller with each advance in technology. While the largeness of skyscrapers make the spectator feel dwarfed before technology, the very same size make the same people feel strong since it is some other people who were able to construct a building of that size. Likewise the use of technology in making peoples' lives easier make the users feel bigger because they give the sense that humankind is capable of living better. Mumford is right in saying that the skyscraper socially enhances American weaknesses, but the skyscraper also shows America's imaginative and corporate power.

Mumford also criticizes American architect Henry Louis Sullivan's, who is considered to be the greatest of skyscraper designers, assertion that a skyscraper should be "lofty" and should be a "proud and soaring thing." Sullivan in his answer to the question of what a skyscraper is or what the chief characteristic of the tall office building is writes in his "The Tall Office Building Artistically Considered" published in *Lippincott's Magazine* as early as 1896:

> [I]t is lofty. This loftiness is to the artist-nature its thrilling aspect. It is the very open organ-tone in its appeal. It must be in turn the dominant chord in his expression of it, the true excitant of his imagination. It must be tall, every inch of it tall. The force and power of altitude must be in it, the glory and pride of exaltation must be in it. It must be every inch a proud and soaring thing, rising in sheer exultation from bottom to top. It is a unit without a single dissenting line, -that it is the new, the unexpected, the eloquent peroration of most bold, most sinister, most forbidding conditions (566).

Agitated by Sullivan's description of a skyscraper as something that should be lofty, Mumford writes in *The Brown Decades*:

> More than anything, the mischief lay in the notion that on the foundation of practical needs the skyscraper could or should be translated into a "proud and soaring thing." This was giving the skyscraper a spiritual function to perform: whereas, in actuality, height in skyscrapers meant either a desire for centralized administration, a desire to increase ground rents, a desire for advertisement, or all three of these together – and none of these functions determines a "proud and soaring thing" (153).

Mumford seems to be criticizing Sullivan's marriage of materialism to idealism and his attempt to attach the skyscraper an inherent sublimity. All the same Sullivan understood the symbolic possibilities of the tall building; for him it was not the technology of tall buildings but the idea of soaring verticality that gave the skyscraper its rationale and its magic. Like Sullivan, Mumford too takes the technology used in the skyscrapers as something not necessarily distinguishing, but on a more pragmatic level he lays out a reductionist view of the skyscraper as something merely a commercial capitalist enterprise driven by the desire for a centralized administration. It is not difficult to see that Mumford disliked the skyscraper in that they undermined human contact: "in the form it had taken, the skyscraper was an *antisocial* conception" (1972 21) [emphasis mine].

If Mumford had disliked the skyscraper, Henry James hated them. James, writing after his move to Great Britain in the mid-1870s returns to New York after a 20-year absence in *The American Scene* (1907), calls the skyscrapers *terrible* "monsters of the mere market" (422). James argues that skyscrapers "are triumphant payers of dividends; all with uncontested and unabashed pride" (419). Not surprisingly even in 1907 the skyscraper is "the element that looms largest" (422) in the cityscape.

James hated the skyscrapers because, according to him they, for example, "cruelly overtopped" and made the "beauty" of Trinity Church so "barely distinguishable" (420). Built in 1846 by Richard Upjohn, the gothic Trinity Church was the tallest building in New York, following the example of medieval cities where the highest building or landmark structure was the cathedral. However in 1892, George B. Post built the Pulitzer Building up to 309 feet, 25 feet higher than Trinity Church, dwarfing the building dedicated to God. "Cathedrals were built because at that time a great church was the symbol of the community in the hands of God" (Gottmann 196). Essentially, the cathedral was a kind of meeting house for believers in the Christian God and the skyscraper was a kind of meeting place for the business. In the skyscraper business overshadowed religion, with the skyscraper the private enterprise or American capitalism found its proud, artistic, and necessarily challenging voice.

> Crowned not only with no history, but with no credible possibility of time for history, and consecrated by no uses save the commercial at any cost, they [skyscrapers] are simply the most piercing notes in that concert of the expensively provisional into which your supreme sense of New York resolves itself. They never begin to speak to you, in the manner of the builded majesties of the world as we have heretofore known such—towers or temples or fortresses or palaces—with the authority of things of permanence or even of things of long duration. One story is good only till another is told, and sky-scrapers are the last word of economic ingenuity only till another word be written (James 420).

In the passage James disagrees with Sullivan who had written that "the design of the tall office building takes its place with all other architectural types made when architecture was a living art. Witness the Greek temple, the Gothic cathedral, the mediaeval fortress. [I]t is evident that *we are merely speaking a foreign language with a noticeable American accent*" (570) [emphasis mine]. What Sullivan is underlying is that the skyscraper form is a continuation of monumental buildings of the past only made modern by the technological progress. It is significant to remember that the city and its built environment are contingent textures, and monuments in these webs of signification constitute the strong points, anchors of such webs:

> A monumental work [has] a *horizon of meaning*: a specific or indefinite multiplicity of meanings, a shifting hierarchy in which now one, now another meaning comes momentarily to the fore, by means of – and for the sake of – a particular action. The social and political operation of a monumental work traverses the various "systems" and "subsystems", or codes and subcodes, which constitute and found the society concerned. But it also surpasses such codes and subcodes, and implies a "supercoding", in that it tends towards the all-embracing presence of totality. To the degree that there are traces of violence and death, negativity and aggressiveness in social practice, the monumental work erases them and replaces them with a tranquil power and certitude which can encompass violence and terror. Thus the mortal "moment" (or component) of the sign is temporarily abolished in monumental space (Lefebvre 222).

The important factor is that although the skyscraper derives its prototype from the history of colossal buildings, with its presence it changes the critical outlook on those colossal buildings. The skyscraper might be shaped by the architectural tradition of the past, but at the same time it changes that past too. As Rem Koolhaas writes in *Delirious New York*: "The contemporary architecture of Manhattan does not consist of the production of new Parthenons but of the pilferage of all useful elements of past 'Parthenons,' which are then reassembled and wrapped around steel skeletons" (110). Likewise, the great surrealist Salvador Dali sees the same historical connection between New York's skyscrapers and colossal pyramids of ancient Egypt. Dali writing during his first visit to New York in his pamphlet "New York Salutes Me!" (1941) says: "New York, you are an Egypt! But the Egypt turned inside out. [...] She erected pyramids of slavery to death, and you erect pyramids of democracy with the vertical organ pipes of your skyscrapers all meeting at the point of infinity of liberty!"

The question of architectural historical continuity and skyscraper aesthetics were also debated back in the nineteenth century. In 1894 an article in *Scribner's* pointed out the inappropriateness of traditional styles for this "new" architectural form: "The Greek temple was a development of the Greek ideal in architecture; the Gothic cathedral was the development of the medieval ideal; the modern office building, if it is to have the rank in architecture to which its importance entitles it, must be the development of modern needs, ideas, necessities" (Ferree 318). On the other hand, James almost disgusted by the eye piercing "novelty" of these giants believes that the practice should be abandoned. However, the evolution of the skyscraper proved James wrong in that "another word" has not been written yet.

One wonders if James had heard that only three years before his death a skyscraper was dubbed a "Cathedral of Commerce." The Woolworth Building (1913) of New York, designed by the famous Cass Gilbert, was made public as the "Cathedral of Commerce," both as a likely union of the almost religious attachment to climbing the social ladder through business and a form that the architect sought to make his product to have the same grandeur of the gothic cathedral.

The owner of the Woolworth Building was a self-made millionaire, Frank Woolworth who was not only determined but obsessed with the idea of building the most superlative building in the world. He wanted to build the most beautiful, the largest, the grandest, the biggest, and of course, the tallest building in the world. Although Woolworth could not secure the necessary financial investment from his bankers, he went on with his project. He paid 13 million dollars in cash in 1913, believing his was a sound investment. The Woolworth Building was opened with an astonishing ceremony: the buildings' 80 thousand lights were lit simultaneously by a signal from President Wilson from the White House to the astonishment of the spectators. The shining example of the "cathedral of commerce" made it clear that Woolworth had created one of the great corporate symbols of his time. In fact, the building was not only a corporate symbol, but the very symbol of the American dream of material success made tangible in the hands of a self-made man. Woolworth was not the last to translate his commercial passions into soaring, prestigious buildings, nor will be real estate mogul Donald Trump (Trump Tower). Even in a city of a skyscraper forest, both individual and corporate passions to assert dominance over the skyline will no doubt go on and indeed is going on. But one needs to be cautious for not reducing the function of the skyscraper only to financial ends:

> The study of the almost volcanic eruption of New York's skyline should not be pursued without a word of caution. Almost anyone can glibly explain the skyline in terms exclusively economic. The narrow island, the great influx of population, the consequent scarcity of land, and as a result the towering buildings – thus runs the argument that is almost universally accepted. Accurate as far as it goes, it has misled countless people into a simple calculation in profit and loss. The development of New York is actually far more enigmatic (*New York Guide* 203).

As enigmatic as it is, many critics of capitalism see the skyscraper form as the arrogant and greedy architectural expression of American pride. One interesting reference comes from a skyscraper entry in the 1954 edition of the *Soviet Encylopedia*, where the skyscraper is condemned both as an architectural style and as a social or economic phenomenon: Here the skyscraper is defined as a multistoried, high building characteristic of American cities and its existence is explained by "the excessive greed of capitalists who want to make the most they can out of a piece of real estate" (quoted in Gottman 192). Another example for the capitalist enthusiasm in the skyscraper form comes with the confessions of an architect: Philip Johnson. Johnson is known for his so-called postmodernist renderings of the skyscraper form in service of corporate capitalism. David Harvey in *The Condition of Postmodernity* quotes Johnson, the architect of AT & T building in New York as saying, "AT & T insisted they wanted something other than just another glass box. We were looking for something that projected the company's image of nobility and strength. No material does that better than granite" (114). Harvey concludes that even if the cost of granite is double the cost of glass, this choice of material to reflect the "nobility and strength" (pride) of the company is something that can be seen through the symbolic function embedded in skyscrapers' capitalist ethos:

> [t]he increasing affluence, power, and authority emerging at the other end of the social scale produces an entirely different ethos. For while it is hard to see that working in the postmodern AT & T building by Philip Johnson is any different from working in the modernist Seagram building by Mies van der Rohe, the image projected to the outside is different. [...] With luxury housing and corporate headquarters, aesthetic twists become an expression of class power (Harvey 114).

According to Harvey where corporate capital was in command (especially in the United States), it could happily appropriate architectural practice to continue building monuments that soared ever higher as symbols of corporate power. Skyscraping monuments like the Rockefeller Center or World Trade Center of New York are a part of "a continuous history of celebrating supposedly sacred class power that brings us in more recent times to the Trump Tower or the postmodernist monumentalism of Philip Johnson's AT & T building" (Harvey 71). Harvey's Marxist rendering of the corporate towers goes hand in hand with Sullivan's most famous quote of all architectural history in this context: *"form ever follows function,* and this is the law" (Sullivan 569).

With the motto *"form ever follows function,"* Sullivan is speaking of the expressive relations of form and structure in nature and in art, thus marking his position in founding modern functionalism. Any part of a building is to be so designated to express the function that it performs within a building; that is to say, a weight bearing beam is to look like a weight bearing beam. This stance marks a shift in architectural thinking, away from ornament.

The function of the corporate tower is one that forwards the domination of the bourgeoisie, and the only way to assert this domination of the capitalist order, the built form has to be extraordinarily large or tall to make it obvious to the eye of the common people. In this respect skyscrapers follow the rationale for building large cathedrals to assert the smallness of the people before the rule of God. Only this time God becomes one of financial power and domination; hence Mammon. Further, this makes Woolworth's nickname, "cathedral of commerce" more plausible and Sullivan's credo is translated into "form follows finance." This is truer for New York than anywhere else in the world, since the United States became more and more powerful economically especially after the world wars skyscraper building skyrocketed in New York. And New York became an ideal city:

> For we have been told by architectural historians that American architecture in this interwar period [between World War I and II] finally created a style of its own when the city was catapulted into being a world-class financial capital. New York, *The Nation* proclaimed in 1929, became the 'mecca and the model' for all of America. Its spectacle of power could be viewed by every passenger who entered the harbor of the city, for its skyscraper towers were a vision 'prophetic of modernity, of immense mechanical superiority, of intolerance of all that is not the newest, the latest and best.' Public grandeur became a by-product of America's commercial architecture whose tone was established in the 1920s (Boyer 463).

Form follows function or finance; or in many ways the two become intertwined. Because as Ada Louise Huxtable, the famous architecture critic, writes there is something unique to architecture: the direct connection between the bases of power and extremely lucrative work. Huxtable carries out a detailed research and criticism in the evolution of the skyscraper form in her *The Tall Building Artistically Reconsidered: The Search for a Skyscraper Style* (1984). Huxtable's work is an acknowledged homage to Sullivan's 1896 essay "The Tall Office Building Artistically Considered" and while leaving out much that has to do with the cultural underpinnings of the skyscraper form (save a little in the introduction), it offers an excellent view of the stylistic changes that the tall building has gone through. Huxtable maintains that the history of the skyscraper is also a history of the twentieth century and it is essentially a search for identity in its stylistic development (102). She identifies four significant phases in the evolution of the skyscraper looking at the whole historical spectrum of the skyscraper design: 1) the functional (early), 2) the eclectic, 3) the modern, 4) the postmodern (13).

Huxtable sees the first skyscrapers (functional) as an economic phenomenon since business was the driving force that called for innovation: "The patron was the investment banker and the muse was cost-efficiency" (14). A typical example for these types of skyscrapers would be the "Republic Building" in Chicago (Holabird and Roche, 1905-1909). The second phase (eclectic) produced some of the skyscraper's most remarkable monuments carrying past forms such as the gothic to heavens like the Woolworth Building in New York (Cass Gilbert 1913) (16). The skyscrapers of the modern phase were a radical break from the past (like everything else that has to do with modernism) and they were seen as a creative challenge that required an original response to technological and cultural change (18) as once was displayed by the twin towers of World Trade Center (Minoru Yamasaki 1973). Finally, the postmodern skyscraper loosened modernist strictures and history or nostalgia became prominent again (20) like Philip Johnson's AT & T Building (1983) in New York.

All the same Huxtable acknowledges the fact that architecture, like other arts, has not been free from the ideological and financial politics: In its most familiar and exhilarating aspect, the skyscraper has been a celebration of modern building technology. But it is just as much a product of zoning and tax law, the real-estate and money markets, code and client requirements, energy and aesthetics, politics and speculation. Not least is the fact that it is the biggest investment game in town (8).

Huxtable too sees the skyscraper and the twentieth century as synonyms, and that the skyscraper is the landmark of twentieth century:

> For the skyscraper is not only the building of the century, it is also the single work of architecture that can be studied as the embodiment and expression of much that makes the century what it is. Today's tall building is a puzzling and paradoxical package. Its standardized, characterless, impersonal space creates the recognizable, charismatic

monuments and the enduring image of twentieth-century cities. For better or for worse, it is measure, parameter, or apotheosis of our consumer and corporate culture. No other building type incorporates so many of the forces of the modern world, or has been so expressive of changing belief systems and so responsive to changing tastes and practices. It romanticizes power and the urban condition and celebrates leverage and cash flow. Its less romantic side effects are greed and chaos writ monstrously large. The tall building probes our collective psyche as it probes the sky (11).

According to Huxtable the skyscraper is this century's most stunning architectural phenomenon since as a structural marvel it breaks the traditional limits on humankind's persistent ambition to build to the heavens: "It is certainly its most overwhelming architectural presence. Shaper of cities and fortunes, it is the dream, past and present, acknowledged or unacknowledged, of almost every architect. From the Tower of Babel onward, the fantasies of builders have been vertical rather than horizontal (Huxtable 7).

This continuous effort to build vertically is what Roland Barthes calls in his *The Eiffel Tower and Other Mythologies* (1997), "a true Babel complex" (7). Therefore what the Turkish poet Enis Batur says in "The Tower of Joyce" (1996), his preface to the Turkish translation of *Ulysses*, which begins at Dublin's Martello Tower, is more than relevant:

> In all monotheistic religions the temples are built in accordance with the principle of height: The topos of worship is held stronger, grander than the other examples of civic architecture, and what is underlined is the fact that real Power belongs to the heavens. [...] Babel is indeed a *key* symbol: In it the *collective* vanity of mankind is defined. To this end, the Tower is a sign of transgression (11) [my translation].

Indeed Huxtable, Barthes and Batur allude to the Biblical Tower of Babel. The "son of man" is condemned to an eternal communication breakdown in the story of the Tower of Babel in *Genesis*:

Now the whole earth had one language and one speech. [...] And they said to one another, 'Come, let us make bricks, and make them thoroughly.' They had brick for stone, and they had asphalt for mortar. And they said, 'Come, let us build ourselves a city, and a *tower, whose top is in the heavens*; let us make a name for ourselves, lest we be scattered abroad over the face of the whole earth'" (11: 1-9) [New King James translation; emphasis mine].

But then God comes down to see the city and the tower, which the sons of men had built, and he punishes or corrects the attempt at unity in human pride by confusing the language of men. Whether or not they could actually build a tower that would reach unto heaven, God takes their activity as an attempt to grasp greatness, rather than waiting for God's blessing. God seems to be offended at their plan because it seems as if they are trying to become gods unto themselves by reaching heaven on their own. Further, as proven by the evolution, and further the domination of the skyscraper towers, especially in the Manhattan skyline, sons and daughters continue to challenge the perceived dominion of God. However, if one takes the Tower of Babel as an archetype for the modern skyscraper much is lost through establishing a single source, not to mention a religious one. This would mean stripping of the skyscraper form's historical evolution, putting it on a transhistorical plane. The evolution of the skyscraper form is much more contingent. This fact calls for a historicist reading of the skyscraper.

Then setting the context for the emergence of the skyscraper form in economic, cultural (symbolic), and spatial factors is needed. At the end of the nineteenth century when the skyscraper as a form was born, the process of industrialization and urbanization reached its heights in New York City. Since the beginning of the nineteenth century, New York was the largest city in the United States, and it was also the center of manufacture and a leading seaport. New York City's geographical location between the Hudson River on the West and the Atlantic Ocean on the East made it the main commercial link to Europe, and the completion of the Erie Canal offered the city a major link to the interior (Adams 44). Also the railroads brought together the initial advantage: "By 1860, New York was in direct contact by rail and telegraph with every major city of the North. By then, it had become the dynamo of the emerging urban system of cities and towns in the Northeast and Middle West which was working a fundamental change in American life (Spann 417). Because of its naturally deep safe harbor New York always dominated the import trade, and with advanced transportation it had large access to natural resources. All these contributed to its evolution as a major center. The combination of trade and manufacturing led to New York's inevitable dominance in the financial world.

New York's financial dominance was also a result of its population of bankers and other financial players. In 1890, almost a quarter of all bankers in the United States were living in New York. In contrast, other major cities like Chicago had only seven percent, and Boston three percent. In addition New York had more technical and professional experts than any major city in the United States (Hammack 44-45). These people were innovative and ambitious; they were taking risks, and they were upwardly mobile. But they needed ways to express their wealth and power. One expression was offered by luxury housing with large mansions, and commercial centers made up of marble and granite. The result was Madison Avenue filled with mansions, and Broadway with its architectural grandeur. By the 1870s the traditional brownstone buildings were replaced by buildings coated with marble and granite. Onto this new architecture came the mass of signs and advertisements that continue to haunt the Times Square. The long Broadway is still a scene, but back in the nineteenth century the quantity of wealth invested in there was extraordinary: "[the] great charm, the chief claim of Broadway to its fame, is the extent of its grand display" (McCabe 130).

Another street that deserves attention in the 1860s and 1870s is Wall Street, not because of its architectural beauty but because of its role in the financial activities of the city. Banks and financial players had offices on the Wall Street and the demand for an office space was high:

> Scarcely a house has less than a score of offices within its walls, and some contain at least three as many. Space is valuable, and rents are high in Wall Street, and many of the leading firms in it have to content

themselves with small, dark apartments, which a conscientious man would hesitate to call an "office." The rents paid of such quarters are enormous, and the buildings yield their owners large incomes every year. The streets running into Wall Street, on the right and left, are also occupied for several blocks with the offices of bankers and brokers, and are all included in the general term "Wall Street," or "The Street" (McCabe 258).

Although Wall Street was the locus of economic activity, Broadway became the center of a new and grandiose architecture called the "commercial palace" because it was the widest, longest, and most centrally located street, and therefore the most prominent site in lower Manhattan. It would not make any sense to locate these symbols on narrow streets where they would not have been seen by the public. Weisman writes that the commercial palaces fulfilled a symbolic need:

> [Commercial palaces] symbolized a reaction in taste on the part of a wealthy and elite social class against the staid austerity of earlier republican period. Stewart's Department Store mirrored the rise of a mercantile royalty who no longer were satisfied with shingles and homespun, but who yearned instead for the trappings of nobility. The palace movement was a reflection of this "calico aristocracy" as *Putnam's* called this group. The commercial palace, in other words, was the architectural symbol of the merchant prince (286).

These commercial palaces are like precursors of the early skyscrapers in their function and symbolism.

The skyscraper was also made possible by another American invention –the passenger elevator. The first officially recorded passenger elevator was installed in 1857 by Otis Elevator Company in a fairly high building in New York City. These elevators were hydraulic and their rise was limited to a height of at most twenty stories. To get over with this limit skyscrapers needed the electric elevator which made its appearance in about 1887. From that time on the height to which people could be lifted mechanically was no longer restricted by physical laws, and the sky became the literal limit (Gottman 191).

With the use of elevator, the steel frame, the development of fireproofing techniques, improved plumbing, heating and ventilation systems, and other technical improvements the skyscraper form evolved and the limitless possibility of building tall offered businesspeople a new form of expressing their rise. Tall buildings became the architectural symbol of the economic world:

> But the skyscraper of commerce looms above the university and the art gallery on the horizon line of the city; and the master builder of the skyscraper, the so-called captain of industry, seems to fill the most conspicuous place in the interest and affections of the city's people. For all its facilities and its acquisitions of purely intellectual or educational nature the key-note of the city is taken from its commerce (Van Dyke 15).

Indeed as Ada Louis Huxtable writes in *The Tall Building Artistically Reconsidered*, "with pitifully few exceptions in the past, New York's skyscrapers have never reached for anything but money" (105). The earliest skyscrapers developed out of the mercantile mentality, but they rose to prominence in the age of finance capitalism. The merchants who invested in tall buildings created the symbolism of size and height.

Further, the earliest industry that sought to transfer its need of strong corporate imagery was the communication industry. Especially newspapers that necessarily relied on mass appeal –from the Pulitzer's early buildings to the new *New York Times* tower in Times Square which is still under construction— were among the first to exploit the symbolism embedded in the tall buildings. The popularity of the metropolitan press was attributable to a new market created by "the longing of urban masses for identity" (Barth 59). Out of their promotional motivations and their desire to impress the public, leading newspapers of the time competed with one another in the tallness race. A commentator cynically notes that the newspaper buildings' rise one above the other "in the humorous hope that the public will believe the length of their subscription lists is in proportion to the height of their towers" (Davis 588). The association became less strong as other industries –like the life insurance industry- began to build skyscrapers, but the association with "big money" never lost its influence.

Indeed, architectural historians cannot agree as to whether which life insurance company building is the first true skyscraper: Home Life Insurance Company Building (Chicago) or Equitable Life Insurance Company Building (New York). Insurance companies needed structures that could embody the seemingly gigantic economic power of their corporations. Morton Keller, an historian of the industry, logically assumes that the presidents of the early life insurance companies had a great consciousness of place and they looked for, and indeed found in elaborate home offices, "the sort of physical expression that their un-material business otherwise denied them" (39). Keller quotes one insurance president as saying that the purpose of these tall buildings was "inspiring local pride, getting a local hold, securing the local business" (39). As the economy shifted from the productive to the non-productive ("unmaterial"), the nature of the business somehow forced the leaders in the market to assert their companies' affluence, and strength in a tangible built form. And the insurance industry, among others, built skyscrapers to create structures that were symbols of their power and nobility and that acted as advertisements to a mass audience.

White-collar class worked for the non-productive sector, or the modern industrial economy. Mostly doing paperwork, these white-collar workers needed to work in close proximity and skyscrapers provided a lot of offices in the same building. Further, owners of the companies gave their names to the buildings, thereby establishing the association of tallness, or verticality with wealth and power: wealthy businessman "built his corporate and commercial buildings as monuments to, and advertisements of, himself. While the culture elite were competing for Old Master paintings, the emergent titans of industry were competing for preeminence on the urban horizon" (Rubin 342).

The increasing number of skyscrapers at the end of the nineteenth century prompted a general recognition of the changing shape of Manhattan. The unique vertical dimension of New York became a source of pride as *King's Handbook of New York City* states as early as 1893: "No metropolis in the civilized world shows such an aggregation of magnificent office-buildings in the same small area of territory as are to be found between the Battery and City-Hall Park" (819).

By the end of 1890s New York City had already become a city of skyscrapers. Manhattan's famous skyline was beginning to be forming. Because of the abundance of skyscrapers a person in Manhattan cannot grasp the overall image of the city, therefore attempts to totalize the whole of the city in one glance were needed and the skyline views offered that chance. Ironically a spectator has to be *outside* the city (preferably on the other side of the Hudson, in New Jersey for example) to see the city. However, as a symbol the skyline is more like a presentation of New York:

> For the purposes served by the symbol, however, it is not really necessary for anyone literally to see the view itself – the important thing is to be able to understand what it represents. The massed buildings, the solidity and density of the agglomeration, the gleaming roofs, the spacious neatness and order that a far view lends the scene, seem to reflect all the energy, the crowdedness, the opulence and magnificence of the city. The skyline represents, in effect, the essence of New York, the great metropolis; New York, as the "greatest" and "richest" city in the world (Strauss 11).

Especially with the advance of cinema New York's skyline became a universal symbol and this represents a major development in the symbolization of New York's verticality. In the early skyline views the skyscrapers came to be seen as the first original products of a new civilization in the new world; a new civilization was in every way American. Therefore, the skyscrapers came also symbolic of American characteristics. According to architectural historian Montgomery Schuyler, the most distinctive thing about the skyscrapers was "the tremendously, the almost awfully impressive expression they give of human energy and of American individualism" (255).

Strong investment in individualism is one of the most definitive elements of American culture and this individualism resonates well with the frontier of the American West. Frederick Jackson Turner defined and formulated the idea of the American Frontier in a speech at the World's Columbian Exhibition back in 1893 in what was to become his famous *The Significance of the Frontier in American History* (1921):

> American social development had been continually beginning over again at the frontier. This perennial rebirth, this fluidity of American life, this expansion westward with its new opportunities, its continual touch with the simplicity of primitive society, furnish the forces dominating American character. The true point of view in the history of this nation is not the Atlantic coast, it is the Great West (2-3).

However, the idea of the frontier does not only lie within the boundaries of the West. Turner concludes that the frontier is much more than a line on the map. He uses an analogy comparing the once-inert continent with a living organism with its "nervous system" alive, changing, growing and evolving from the perspective of its expanding frontier line. Its progress is a "perennial rebirth," for each time the frontier advances, the original encounter between "civilization" and wilderness is reproduced and the original challenges are again to be met. Frontiersman has to wrap himself up in a new identity; he has to become self-reliant. Therefore, he has to explore the brave and strong self hidden in him. To cope with the improvisatory aspects of wilderness, he becomes a supreme individualist: "he eschews both authority and society if he feels choked by them" (Simonson 10-11). With each renewal of the frontier experience, qualities such as restlessness, inventiveness, self-confidence, optimism, and being enormously energetic nurtures the pioneers in their adventure.

The important element is the sense of adventure, the desire to conquer the unknown. "Go west, young man, and grow up with the country" said journalist John B. L. Soule in 1851 but it was another journalist Horace Greely who had popularized the motto and fuelled the desires of expansion. A few decades later the very same motto would be translated into "Go *up* young man, and grow up with the country" in the form of early skyscrapers. Just as once West was the unknown, and was conquered and "Americanized" by the pioneers, the "new" frontier came with the skyscraper form in New York where art (architecture) and finance (business) conquered the heavens: "In other words: Manhattan has no choice but the skyward extrusion of the Grid itself; only the Skyscraper offers business the wide-open spaces of a man-made Wild West, a *frontier in the sky*" (Koolhaas 87). Patriotism and the rediscovery of the power of the frontier contributed to the creation of the skyscraper. Since the frontier ideal denies a history and claims self-reliant individualism, the skyscraper rose on the shoulders of those self-made individuals to claim the sky.

Howard Roark (Gary Cooper), the hero of the film *The Fountain Head* (1949) is one of the best examples for this type of "vertical" pioneer. Directed by King Vidor, the film -adopted from the novel by the same title, by the hard-line individualist Ayn Rand who also wrote the screenplay- depicts a self-taught architect who is strong, rugged and independent just like the pioneers.

Howard Roark is a daring modern architect and is struggling to build his extraordinary designs. His rival, Peter Keating (Kent Smith) is a man of conventions who designs neoclassical skyscrapers and is very successful. However, when Keating feels that his success has come to a halt he calls Roark to design a housing project to be submitted under his name. Roark agrees, since he knows that using once successful Keating's name would be much more advantageous than using his own. But when Roark sees that his design has been radically changed during construction he makes the buildings explode with dynamites causing widespread anger. Eventually he wins the trial and is acquitted. Not surprisingly, in the end of the film he is building "the tallest skyscraper" in the world. With Roark's amazing success it becomes clear that Rand seeks to present an allegory or a parable of ideas using the clash of architectural modernism against the older eclectic, neoclassical architecture to exemplify her belief in individualism (Sanders 126-131). Interestingly almost everyone in the film, except Roark, is either weak or completely evil.

Roark is successful in the end, and the teachings of his mentor, a legendary modern architect Henry Cameron (Henry Hull) has invaluable influence on him. Cameron speaks of the skyscrapers as he is taken to hospital by an ambulance, Roark listening:

> Skyscrapers, the greatest structural invention of man! Yet they made them look like Greek temples, Gothic cathedrals, and mongrels of every ancient style they could borrow. I told them that the form of a building was to follow its function! That new materials demand new forms! That one building can't borrow pieces of another's shape, just as one man can't borrow another's soul.

Cameron in this speech clearly echoes Sullivan (*"form ever follows function"*). With Cameron's words the film openly takes sides with the modernist individual who breaks all ties with the collective past. In another instance, newspaper mogul Gail Wynand (Raymond Massey) dismisses neoclassical skyscraper designs for his paper's proposed tower as "great big marble bromides." Not only through the dialogues of the characters but also through their visual presence, the skyscrapers dominate the film as the Manhattan skyline penetrates each and every frame.

Although *The Fountainhead* claims a modern New York that is treated as a heaven on earth with no past, Jean Paul Sartre in his "New York, the Colonial City" calls New York "a colonial city, an outpost [...] the most prodigious monument man has ever built to himself" (130). Jean Baudrillard in his *America* writes that New York is a "pharaonic city almost completely made up of standing stones" (46). Or as Marshall Berman writes in *All That is Solid Melts into Air*:

> A great deal of New York's construction and development over the past century needs to be seen as symbolic action and communication: it has been conceived and executed not merely to serve immediate economic and political needs, but at least equally important, to demonstrate to the whole world what modern men can build and how life can be imagined and lived (288-289).

These writers are only a few among a humongous group of intellectuals who had written about New York, but are chosen to demonstrate the city's architectural scene is an essential component of the city that was shaped by as much economic concerns as symbolic concerns. New York City is a "colonial outpost," an ideal example, a demonstration for the rest of the world. As a

45

symbol New York was created by a group of people to communicate an idea to another group of people. The message well-taken is known all over the world now.

2. PSYCHOANALYTIC NEW YORK

> *Cities, like dreams, are made of desires and fears.*
> Italo Calvino, *Invisible Cities*, 1972

> *New York [r]esurrection of the Atlantic Dream, Atlantis of the subconscious.*
> Salvador Dali, "New York Salutes Me!" 1941

Franz Kafka tells a tale about a wall in "The Great Wall of China." This wall is built on suspicion. The wall's effectiveness is doubtful; it is rumored to have gaps, and further its very justification can be questioned. The wall is justified as protection against the "other," the supposedly barbarian hordes of the north, who are depicted as savages "with great pointed teeth." In fact the peoples of the south have no real understanding of these northern "barbarians." If the wall has gaps it is not a sufficient protection against the supposed savages, and the great distance separating the peoples of the south and north would be enough defense in itself. The wall, then, in Kafka's terms, is a wall built on suspicion, whose role, while supposedly being to keep out the "other," is in fact to bond those "protected" by it, and serves as a symbol of allegiance to the emperor (Leach xx). Indeed the very building of the wall unites the people into "a ring of brothers, a current of blood no longer confined within the narrow circulation of one body, but sweetly rolling and yet ever returning throughout the endless leagues of China" (Kafka 238). The wall while separating the peoples of the south and the north, also unites those who built them acting as a physical manifestation of a social order. It offers a sense of collective identity, and security to peoples of the south who are enclosed within its boundaries, but it at the same time makes the peoples of the north "others" from whom the southerners need to be protected. The wall then becomes an agent of power relations between the peoples, excluding the perceived other socially, psychologically and physically.

Kafka's tale about the separation of the territory and peoples, the demonized other and sense of self and space provides a good example for a psychoanalytic rendering of the dynamics between space, the built environment and the human psyche. The story of the wall is in fact a complex narrative of the ways in which perceptions of space and self intermingle. Therefore, psychoanalysis with its research program into the ways in which people gain a sense of who they are coincides perfectly with the ways in which built environment is mediated and which helps tell people their own place in the world as well as the other's place, and the interaction between.

The images of the built environment are products of desires and needs of the human subject or groups conscious or otherwise. From the view of psychoanalysis the world of dreams is at the same time a real world where distinctions between the imagined and the real dissolve since unconscious processes lie beneath the personal, the social and the spatial. As Siegfried Kracauer writes:

> Each typical space is brought into being by typical social relations that, without the distorting intervention of consciousness, express themselves in it. Everything that is disowned by consciousness, everything that would otherwise be intentionally overlooked, contributes to its construction. Spatial images are the dreams of society. Wherever the hieroglyphics of any spatial image are deciphered, there the basis of social reality presents itself (1997 60).

Psychodynamics of space, the relationship between the subject, the society and the built environment, then, will reveal a complex web of discourses founded on the relationship not just between the individual and her/his internal world and external world but those between meaning, identity and power. This is a critically contingent field connecting the internal world (psyche) of the subject with the external physical world (the built environment) of a collection of subjects forming a society. This chapter offers a research into the psychodynamics of the skyscraper form in American society exemplified through the immensely vertical architectural layout in New York City through a dialogue between psychoanalysts Sigmund Freud and Jacques Lacan, and Marxist sociologist Henri Lefebvre (1901-1991) who draws heavily on Freudian and Lacanian psychoanalysis in his analysis of the production of space, and the oppressive skyscrapers of John Dos Passos's (1896-1970) *Manhattan Transfer*.

However, this is not an attempt to explain a certain social phenomenon like the skyscraper purely in psychological terms, as Fredric Jameson reminds the readers in his "Imaginary and Symbolic in Lacan: Marxism, Psychoanalytic Criticism, and the Problem of the Subject" (1982) quoting sociologist Emile Durkheim who said "whenever a social phenomenon is directly explained by a psychological phenomenon, we may be sure that the explanation is false" (339). Clearly Jameson shows his opposition, through Durkheim, to an essentialist, teleological approach and the reduction of the social to a psychological essence. Indeed Jameson and Durkheim are right in principle, and in a postmodern world of ever sliding signifiers a tendency to reductionism is way too absurd. Lacan too warns his readers on the same subject in "A Theoretical Introduction to the Functions of Psychoanalysis in Criminology" saying "we must, with the utmost rigor, distinguish from psychoanalytic theory the constant fallacious attempts to base on analytic theory notions such as those of a model personality, a national character, or a collective superego" (16). However, it is hard to find a text that has anything to do with a social phenomenon and is not contaminated with at least a slight reductionism; accordingly each social theorist to date has been accused of mere essentialism, creating "grand narratives" thereby contributing to the status quo from Marx to Freud, to Lacan, from Foucault to Bourdieu, even to Lyotard himself. This may be an ill of the nature of all social sciences at one point, but a text on the skyscraper phenomenon, though recognizing the contingent web of discourses that helps form it, falls into some sort of essentialism for basic purposes of limitation.

Further, Freudian and Lacanian psychoanalysis is compatible with the resistances to psychological reductionism because it underlines the relational tensions between the subject and the built environment. This study attempts to avoid that sort of essentialism in establishing a dialogue of the psychoanalytic (Freud and Lacan) with the social (Foucault and Bourdieu) in laying out the complex web of discourses in and around which the skyscraper phenomenon is built. Because as the skyscraper as a form came into being on the objective level of the social (need -economic push for frugal land use; political and financial power embedded in tallness; concentration of workers in a single tall building thereby altering spatial organization of power relations), it also assumes a subjective level (desire -the self-made investor and architect's ego; aggression, the alienated subject). Ada Louis Huxtable underlines the individual level, though she simply posits a romantic, humanist and essentialist look on the urge to build tall:

> "[t]here are other, less pragmatic factors that influence the decision to build tall, of which much is usually made. The desire to convey image, status, power, and prestige, to signal economic or cultural dominance, is universally acknowledged. Not least—although it is seldom discussed in the corridors of corporate or political power— is the architect's desire to create a museum-worthy object, usually against considerable odds; it is the *artist's ego-play* against the builder's. The drive for *immortality*; or at least for the accolades of the art establishment, is always present. There is, finally, the basic human desire to build to the very limits of strength and knowledge to achieve the limits of the achievable. This is the ultimate, eternal, irresistible challenge" (99) [emphasis mine].

While specific economic and cultural reasons that gave way to the skyscraper have been taken into consideration in the first chapter; New York businesspeople, architects, urban planners, political leaders, last but not least New Yorkers themselves or American society at large cannot be rendered as a patient lying on the psychoanalyst's couch having a collective superego or a collective unconscious that is suffering from an incurable psychopathologic narcissism in the skyscrapers' ever upward thrust in a pure display of economic power. But this is not to say that a common ideal –asserting the individualistic characteristic of the society— was not at play. This would also be going against Freud who wrote in *Civilization and Its Discontents* (1930) that the past of a city (Rome in his case) cannot be compared with the past of the mind and a city is "*a priori* unsuited for a comparison of this sort with a mental organism" (19). Freud initially asks "by a flight of imagination" what would have happened if Rome was not "a human habitation but a psychical entity with a similarly long and copious past" (18). Then he reasons this is not a suitable comparison since although the assumption that everything past is preserved in mental life only on the condition that the organ of the mind remains intact and that its tissues are not damaged by trauma or inflammation holds true, destructive influences like these sicknesses (raids-actual or imaginary- by the enemy for example) are ever present in the history of a city (19). On the city and the psyche Lefebvre also points out that assuming the city has a collective unconscious life would be misleading. He writes in *The Production of Space*, although extensively depending on psychoanalytic concepts, that psychoanalysis would only be revitalized if it could only be proved that the city has an unconscious life: "If it turned out, for instance, that every society, and particularly (for our purposes) the city, had an underground and repressed life, and hence an 'unconscious' of its own, there can be no doubt that interest in psychoanalysis, at present on the decline, would get a new lease on life" (36). Explaining everything purely in terms of the unconscious undoubtedly leads to reductionism, since historical facts also shape the perception and the creation of both space and the individual. For Lefebvre what matters is "to expound the process of production" of space (36), for this study at hand what matters is to expound the processes of reproduction of spatial power relations exemplified through the skyscrapers of New York.

Civilization and Its Discontents is not the only work by Freud that engages in a psychoanalytic socio-political analysis. He had written on the issue most notably in *Group Psychology and the Analysis of the Ego* (1921), in *The Future of an Illusion* (1927) as well as in his short piece "Why War?" (1933). Moreover, as Lacan himself points out in "The Freudian Thing, or the Meaning of the Return to Freud in Psychoanalysis" (1955), Freud regards the study of the social (language, institutions, literature, art) as a necessary prerequisite for the understanding of the psychoanalytic experience itself:

> We need but thumb through the pages of Freud's work for it to become abundantly clear that he regarded a history of languages [*langue*] and institutions, and the resonances—whether attested to or not in human memory—of literature and of the significations involved in works of art, as necessary to an understanding of the text of our experience; indeed, Freud himself found his inspiration, ways of thinking, and arsenal of

techniques therein. But he also believed it wasn't superfluous to make them a condition for instituting the teaching of psychoanalysis (136).

Lacan also adds that it is important to "avoid social-psychological objectification" (136). However Freud and Lacan handle the relation of the individual and social levels quite differently in some respects. Freud argues just at the beginning of *Group Psychology and the Analysis of the Ego* that there is no contrast between individual psychology and social (group) psychology: "In the individual's mental life someone else is invariably involved, as a model, as an object, as a helper, as an opponent; and so from the very first individual psychology, in this extended but entirely justifiable sense of the words, is at the same time social psychology as well" (3). Lacan agrees with Freud that the social can be analyzed by psychoanalysis, but he does not think it is rational to reduce the social to an individual level. Lacan rather propounds a confluence between them:

> It may be well that since its experience is limited to the individual, psychoanalysis cannot claim to grasp the totality of any sociological object, or even the entirety of causes currently operating in our society. Even so, in its treatment of the individual, psychoanalysis has discovered relational tensions that appear to play a fundamental role in all societies, as if the discontent in civilisation went so far as to reveal the very joint of nature to culture. If one makes the appropriate transformation, one can extend the formulas of psychoanalysis concerning this joint to certain human sciences that can utilise them (1996 14).

It is also important to acknowledge one fact, that neither Freud nor Lacan were political theorists, they were first of all psychoanalysts who drew their basic categories and theoretical frames primarily form their clinical experiences. Nevertheless, insofar as Freudian and Lacanian psychoanalysis interconnect the internal mental world of people with the external world of society (and nature), they offer indispensable insights into the relation between people and the built environment.

2.1. The Freudian Subject and the Built Environment

A study of the relation between people and the built environment necessitates first of all defining who these people are. An account of the Freudian subject is therefore necessary.

Freud is a revolutionary theorist of psychology and culture and, especially, of the relation between psychology and culture. Freud's research program was revolutionary because it showed the relationship between the individual and society as it underlined the insidious transformation of external social codes into internal, psychological, individual ones by a symbolically violent fashion. Cultural historian Eli Zaretsky writes: "[Freud's] most important idea was that socially imposed categories and distinctions dissolve within the individual and are remade as the individual's own unique wishes" (72). The revolution lies in his account of the dissolution of external social codes and their reformulation as internal or psychological. Therefore, Freudian psychoanalysis is an indispensable tool in getting to understand the unconscious controlling mechanisms that are constantly at work both in the human mind and social life.

Equally important is the fact that Freud's works are at the bottom all about control. Especially in his later works, such as *Civilization and Its Discontents*, *Group Psychology and the Analysis of the Ego*, he thought about subjective and social control mechanisms and the ways in which they shape one another[3].

According to Freudian psychoanalytic theory, the human mind operates in a way to ensure the control of human instincts. Just like the human mind, the

---

[3] The crucial binding theory that brings together psychoanalysis and Bourdieu's sociology is the concept of symbolic power and the violence that emanates from it. The insidiousness of the transformation, and the very fact that it "dissolves," becomes invisible is what makes it just as threatening as physical violence. Bourdieu's notion of "symbolic violence" or "symbolic power" is discussed in detail in the following chapter. In turn psychoanalysis as a critical theory of society challenges the forms of domination in its research into the said controlling mechanisms.

society also has its own social superego to guarantee the mass control of those who are a part of that society. However, these individual and social superegos are not two distinct, unrelated mechanisms; they are in a constant, inseparable interaction. Freud saw an analogy between the advent of civilization and the development of the human mind, acknowledging the formation of a social or cultural superego. He writes in *Civilization and Its Discontents*: "It can be asserted that the community, too, evolves a super-ego under whose influence cultural development proceeds" (106). Therefore, architecture, one of the first cultural developments that humankind had achieved in building the first house to protect itself from the hostile environment (wild animals, climate, etc.) is already implicated in the "formation" of this social superego.

The modern individual is under the pressure of her/his superego which is already social since social and psychological processes reinforce each other. S/he has to cope with the restrictions imposed on her/him by sacrificing her/his primary libidinal instincts, or by indulging them as superego; that is to say, her/his instincts aiming to satisfy the pleasure principle are replaced by the reality principle "under the influence of the ego's instincts of self-preservation" (Freud, 1920 7). This is necessary if s/he wants to avoid unpleasure or live in harmony with others in society.

The individual has to cope with inner and outer forces which direct her/him in her/his relations with herself/himself and with other people. The interaction between these forces is basically one of conflict. Freud lays out the inner conflict where the leading roles are shared by love and life (Eros, life instincts), and aggression and death (Thanatos, death instincts) in a lifelong struggle for dominance in his *Beyond the Pleasure Principle* (1920). An insight into how death instincts came to occupy such a great role in the human mind necessitates conditioning them in relation to the life instincts. In the essential dualism of his final version of the instinct theory Freud maintains that the life instincts do not only include the sexual instincts but also the instincts of self-preservation (1920 63). Therefore one can conclude that the life instincts are those that aim at keeping the individual alive. Sexual instincts "are perpetually attempting and achieving a renewal of life," says Freud, whereas death instincts tend toward destruction and they "seek to lead what is living to death" (1920 55). Freud attaches great importance to death instincts, especially the ways in which they manifest themselves as turning towards external objects in the form of aggression and consequently their desired suppression by culture. He also propounds a solution for this in *Civilization and Its Discontents* where aggression becomes central to the creation of the superego —as violence turned back against itself.

Also in *Totem and Taboo* (1913) Freud lays out an account of the roots of aggression in civilized life. Alongside aggression, prohibition in general and specifically the incest taboo are his major concerns in this work. Freud's major guiding idea in this analysis is that society prohibits what its members *really* desire: "The basis of taboo is a prohibited action, for performing which a strong inclination exists in the unconscious" (41). Therefore, incest and murder, which are the two greatest taboo prohibitions that began with civilization and continuing today, correspond to "the oldest and most powerful of human desires" (Freud, 1913 41). Freud analyzes the social structure of his day depending on his own claim that psychically past has never passed. Thus history becomes something alive in the present on which it has a tremendous effect.

Freud's emphasis on the past still living in the present is central in his view of the individual and society. The individual's present mental health and sexual health depend on her/his past, on her/his infantile sexuality, primarily on the Oedipus complex. The same contingency is also true for society, which owes its development to its past achievements and failures, but for Freud all cultural achievements depend on the same beginnings as the individual: "the beginnings of religion, morals, society and art converge in the Œdipus complex" (1913 194). Freud maintains that the Oedipus complex, or a man's ambiguous relation to his father, in that he both loves and hates the father at the same time, displaying an intense emotional ambivalence "lies at the root of many important cultural institutions" (1913 194).

Totem and Taboo presents what is behind the structure of society: It is this horror of incest and behind that horror Freud sees the desire for incest and a great desire to act on that even if it leads to murder. On a structural level, it is any prohibition that creates and created by desire lays the foundations of a society. Therefore, the prohibition of incest is just an example for Freud, though a major one, to forward his analysis of society.

The prohibition of incest is at the root of social control of individual human instincts. Furthermore, Freud suggests that this taboo has come into being because of the feelings of guilt that the brothers have after they kill the primal father. Simply put, the primal father (the leader of the group) is violent and jealous and keeps all the women for himself and drives away his sons when they grow up. The exiled brothers come together and kill their father one day and devour him. In killing the father who had all the power in his hands, the brothers now take over his power. And in devouring him they each assume a portion of his strength and accomplish their identification with him. Only in union are they able to get rid of the father whom they love, hate, and envy and fear so much:

> They hated their father, who presented such a formidable obstacle to their craving for power and their sexual desires; but they loved and admired him too. After they had got rid of him, had satisfied their hatred and had put into effect their wish to identify themselves with him, the affection which had all this time been pushed under was bound to make itself felt. It did so in the form of remorse. A sense of guilt made its appearance which in this instance coincided with the remorse felt by the whole group. *The dead father became stronger than the living one had been...* (Freud, 1913 177-78) [emphasis mine]

This richly suggestive statement not only underlines the brothers' ambivalence towards authority, personified in the father, but also their feelings of guilt in the patricide they had committed which eventually becomes unconscious and finds its place in the social superego. One is inclined to think that the brothers and sisters would change the repressive environment they were forced to live in but strangely, also reasonably enough, after they kill the father they cannot do so because the father in his physical absence becomes more powerful in his psychological presence: "The brothers identify with the father they have killed. [...] The father thus becomes far more powerful in death than in life; it is in death that he institutes human history" (Mitchell

403). They have only one way to avoid self-destruction and they institute the law against incest. They find a solution to suppression only in establishing another inhibition and simply reimpose the father's authority in new forms:

> Psychoanalysis traces the origin of intrapsychic conflict to the condition under which social authority recreates itself in the unconscious mind, and specifically to the institution of the patriarchal family, which crushes the revolt of the son against the father, saddles the son with a guilty conscience, and makes him grow up to become a tyrant in his own right (Lasch 24).

This way they continue to follow the rule of the father by which they have always lived. In this the father becomes the embodiment of the group's superego and also the point of identification for the group. However, Freud's account of the killing of the father is not a set of subject positions but it offers a pattern of symbolic relationships in which the law of the father (the leader, the common ideal, etc.) must be obeyed. Freud does not just offer an essential source for relations; he provides a structure to be followed where there is authority and submission to that authority.

Incest for the primal horde does not essentially mean having sexual intercourse with people who had a blood relationship with one another; rather it signifies the larger family of the horde. The prohibition of incest is linked with totemism since it is a law against the people of the same totem having sexual relations. The totem occupies a significant role as a surrogate for the father. Brothers find the substitute in the totem animal. Thus the taboo on incest becomes one of the main bases that civilization rests upon.

Freud sees that social authority too follows the oedipal pattern, where the child submits to the father's orders and gives up incestuous desires which are directed towards the mother. The father figure also has a social counterpart in that the leader of a group is also a father figure carrying along the oedipal pattern into the social network of relations among the group. "According to Freud, people who have become authorities and elicit obedience from others are to be seen as father figures not only if they impose their laws in the face-to-face politics of their biological families, but also if they rule in the larger sphere of public politics" (Brunner 147).

Moreover, in this antagonism, the pleasure principle which regulates mental events automatically (Freud, 1920 3) plays a decisive role. The pleasure principle maintains that the instincts need to be satisfied through object-cathexes. Freud underlines the importance of the pleasure principle but is careful to state that it is more like a tendency: "[t]here exists in the mind a strong *tendency* towards the pleasure principle, but that tendency is opposed by certain other forces or circumstances, so that the final outcome cannot always be in harmony with the tendency towards pleasure" (1920 6). Although Freud maintains that however strong, the pleasure principle is a tendency in the psyche, he does not minimize its importance and he even qualifies its supreme significance. The "certain other forces or circumstances" that Freud talks about are the ones regulated by the reality principle.

Reality principle is not necessarily antagonistic to the pleasure principle because it does not provide a full obstacle on the way to pleasure. It still has the intention of obtaining pleasure in the end, but it nevertheless demands that an indirect course be taken towards pleasure, putting off satisfaction or in abandonment of some possibilities of satisfaction. With the application of reality-testing by the ego to the demands of the id, the reality principle shows itself. Pleasure principle "as the method of working employed by the sexual instincts" often overcomes the reality principle (Freud, 1920 7). The instincts that seek satisfaction at all costs are under strict scrutiny by the ego, which sees them as incompatible with the reality principle and accordingly, since they are dangerous to the unity and harmony, strives to get rid of them by the process of repression. The repressed material loses its chances for satisfaction. All the same, especially with the sexual instincts, they try to find their way towards satisfaction in disguised forms through roundabout paths. If they succeed in the end, the ego perceives this as one of unpleasure (Freud, 1920 8).

What lies *beyond* the pleasure principle and overrides it is the compulsion to repeat. Clearly seen in infantile psychology, specifically in children's games, the compulsion to repeat is a way of fighting the traumatic experience (mother's absence for example) and "exhibit[s] to a high degree an instinctual character" (Freud, 1920 41). All instinctual impulses affect unconscious mechanisms and instincts which are "the representatives of all the forces originating in the interior of the body and transmitted to the mental apparatus" are related to the compulsion to repeat: "It seems, then, that an instinct is an urge inherent in organic life to restore an earlier state of things which the living entity has been obliged to abandon under the pressure of external disturbing forces" (Freud, 1920 40-43). In keeping the status quo these conservative instincts might pretend that they are after some change or progress while they are in fact looking for paths not unknown to them. However, if the original status quo is one that is inorganic then all instincts tend towards death. Thus life instincts are originally agents of death:

> Another striking fact is that the life instincts have so much more contact with our internal perception—emerging as breakers of the peace and constantly producing tensions whose release is felt as pleasure—while the death instincts seem to do their work unobtrusively. The pleasure principle seems actually to serve the death instincts (Freud, 1920 77).

Freud further expounds his theory of these antagonistic instincts in *The Ego and the Id* (1923) in connection with his now complete "structural theory" of the mind. The structural theory of the mind is essentially the division of the working mechanism of the human mind which Freud divides into three different yet interacting parts: the id, the ego and the superego. As opposed to the id, the ego evolves. It grows out of the id, and indeed part of the ego too will remain unconscious. That people learn how to reason and abide by rules are functions of the ego. The superego on the other hand, grows out of the ego according to one account, acts as a controlling punishment mechanism that directs all its criticism towards the ego. However, since interaction is constantly at work among these three parts, all attempts to define each one with sharp distinctions will prove futile.

Roughly speaking, the id is the store of instincts, the true reservoir of libido (though Freud uses the term for the ego at certain points since libido gets sent out to objects), contains passions and the repressed material, is guided by the pleasure principle and is wholly unconscious. The ego, on the other hand, is guided by the reality principle, by the external world. In its contingent and developmental status, it endeavors to substitute the reality principle for the pleasure principle. The superego (originally the ego ideal) is the critical agency that exercises censorship. It is the seat of morality and conscience; yet significantly the origins of morality lie in aggression. It is the cruel dictator of the human mind who carries out psychological coercion always saying "Thou shalt not." It is only partly conscious since it harbors unconscious feelings of guilt.

The battleground for the conflict between life and death instincts is mainly the id: "[u]nder the domination of the mute but powerful death instincts, which desire to be at peace and (prompted by the pleasure principle) to put Eros, the mischiefmaker, to rest" (Freud, 1923 62). The demands of Eros, which are at heart sexual instincts, are clearly instinctual, but now instinct is torn in two different directions: to slow down the descent into death and destruction by introducing fresh tensions, and producing pleasure. Meanwhile the id, under the guidance of the perception of unpleasures or the pleasure principle, tries to fend off these newly introduced tensions. The ego lends a hand to the id in its struggle to master these tensions by sublimating some of the libido for itself and its purposes (Freud, 1923 46-47). Furthermore, the superego, which is also an outlet for aggressive impulses, is there to punish any wrongdoing that the ego might carry out.

Freud's structural theory of the mind with the hypothesis of the superego explains the workings of the never-ending internal and external conflicts on the part of human beings. In this conflict the ego is threatened by three corresponding dangers: "from the external world, from the libido of the id, and from the severity of the super-ego" (Freud, 1923 58). Freud maintains that the more human beings control their aggressiveness (death instincts) the more intense will be their superegos' inclination to aggressiveness against their egos. The superego is itself simply the diverting back upon the self of primary forces of aggression and destruction, and the superego's aggressiveness towards the ego comes in the form of morality, although the ego itself strives to control instincts, as opposed to the totally amoral id (Freud, 1923 56).

> Towards the two classes of instincts the ego's attitude is not impartial. Through its work of identification and sublimation it gives the death instincts in the id assistance in gaining control over libido, but in so doing it runs the risk of becoming the object of the death instincts and of itself perishing. In order to be able to help in this way it has had itself to become filled with libido; it thus itself becomes the representative of Eros and thenceforward desires to live and to be loved (Freud, 1923 59).

The desire of the ego to be loved finds its way in narcissism where the choice of an object to be loved falls on the person's own body or her/his own ego. The idea of narcissism becomes an essential part of social relations. Freud writes in 1914 "On Narcissism: An Introduction": "For it seems very evident that another person's narcissism has a great attraction for those who have renounced part of their own narcissism and are in search of object-love" (89). Having renounced some of their own narcissism, people find a corollary for that in following leaders who are essentially narcissistic, an idea that Freud analyses in his papers on narcissism, "Mourning and Melancholia" (1917), *Totem and Taboo* (1913) and in a more detailed fashion in *The Group Psychology and the Analysis of the Ego* (1921).

At the same time the superego and its critical agency that Freud introduces for the first time in "On Narcissism: An Introduction" never stops bothering the ego. Linked to the primal narcissism formed in the infantile psyche, the superego keeps attacking the ego's self-respect, establishing itself as a self-observing therefore as a self-critical agent in the mental apparatus. Narcissism contains self-love, auto-erotism in which one treats his own body in the same way as s/he would treat the body of a sexual object. In narcissism the libido is allocated to the ego and thus the ego becomes the venue of object cathexis. Freud asserts that there is an original libidinal cathexis of the ego, and from there some is given off to objects (1914 75). In this way an antithesis between ego-libido and object libido arises, and for people to have healthy mental lives, it is necessary to pass beyond the borders of narcissism and to attach the libido to objects (Freud, 1914 75, 85). Renouncing part of one's own narcissism in favor of a love-object always impoverishes the ego. Then a question arises: why would anyone follow a leader lending a portion of her/his own self-love to that love object in spite of impoverishing her/his own ego? For Freud the answer lies in the paths leading to the choice of an object:

A person may love:--
(1) According to the narcissistic type:
    (a) what he himself is (i.e. himself),
    (b) what he himself was,
    (c) what he himself would like to be,
    (d) someone who was once part of himself.

(2) According to the anaclitic (attachment) type:
    (a) the woman who feeds him,
    (b) the man who protects him,
and the succession of substitutes who take their place (1914 90).

The third article in the narcissistic type and the ones in the "normal" anaclitic type provide the answer why people give in to control and the authority of others. The controlling power of the leader offers the individual a way of cathecting the ego-libido which provides her/him the necessary satisfaction. The individual looks up to the powerful leader as someone he too could have been, whom he would have liked to replace.

Another factor that has an impact on narcissism is what Freud calls the castration complex: "The most significant portion of [the child's original narcissism] can be singled out in the shape of the 'castration complex' (in boys, anxiety about the penis—in girls, envy for the penis" (1914 92). Castration complex centers on the fantasy of castration which is produced in response to the child's puzzlement over the anatomical difference between the sexes –the presence or absence of the penis. The male child (both Freud's and Lacan's child is a boy) thinks that this difference comes from the fact that the girl's penis has been cut off. The structure and consequences of the castration complex are different in the boy and the girl. The boy fears castration, which he sees as the carrying out of a paternal threat made in reply to his sexual activities; the result for him is an intense "castration anxiety." For the boy it marks the terminal crisis of the Oedipus complex in that it has the effect of placing a prohibition upon the child's maternal object; castration anxiety introduces him into the period of latency and precipitates the formation of the superego. In the girl, the absence of a penis is experienced as a wrong suffered which she attempts to deny, to compensate for or to remedy. For the girl it initiates the research which leads her to desire the paternal penis; it thus constitutes the point of entry into the Oedipal phase. The castration complex is closely linked with the Oedipus complex, especially Oedipus complex's prohibitive and normative function (Laplanche and Pontalis 56-57). Freud writes "in the particular field of the castration complex, [...] the two groups of instincts [ego instincts and libidinal instincts] still operating in unison and inseparably mingled, make their appearance as narcissistic interests" (1914 92). In Freud's rendering of the child's original narcissism the phallus is an essential component of the child's self-image. Therefore, any threat to the phallus is a radical danger to this image.

Libidinal instinctual impulses are repressed if they come into conflict with the subject's cultural and ethical ideas: the individual recognizes these ideas "as a standard for himself and submits to the claims that they make on him" (Freud, 1914 93). Repression proceeds from the ego, or more precisely from the self-respect of the ego, in its attempts to avoid unpleasure. The most important factor in this process is the formation of the ego ideal: "We can say that the man has set up an *ideal* in himself by which he measures his actual ego. [...] For the ego the formation of an ideal would be the conditioning factor of repression" (Freud, 1914 94). The ego ideal, as an agency of the personality, results from the union of narcissism (idealization of the ego) and identification with the parents or with their substitutes, or with collective ideals:

> This ideal ego is now the target of the self-love which was enjoyed in childhood by the actual ego. The subject's narcissism makes its appearance displaced on to this new ideal ego, which, like the infantile ego, finds itself possessed of every perfection that is of value. As always

where the libido is concerned, man has here again shown himself incapable of giving up a satisfaction he had once enjoyed. He is not willing to forgo the narcissistic perfection of his childhood; and when, as he grows up, he is disturbed by the admonitions of others and by the awakening of his own critical judgment, so that he can no longer retain that perfection, he seeks to recover it in the new form of an ego ideal. What he projects before him as his ideal is the substitute for the lost narcissism of his childhood in which he was his own ideal" (Freud, 1914 94).

However, this new ideal ego does not only concern the individual her/himself since s/he carries on a "twofold existence:" one to serve her/his own purposes and the other as a link in a chain in society (Freud, 1914 78). Therefore, in *Group Psychology and the Analysis of the Ego* (1921) the role of the ego ideal is central. Freud sees the ego ideal responsible for fascination and submission to leaders, or all cases in which the subject substitutes another person or object for his ego ideal. The object without any change to its nature is idealized and exalted in the subject's mind. For Freud, the ego ideal opens up an important door for understanding group psychology: "In addition to its individual side, this ideal has a social side; it is also the common ideal of a family, a class or a nation" (1914 101).

In *Group Psychology and the Analysis of the Ego*, Freud shows how civilization represses and distorts the expression of human desires, and how people relate to one another and to authority (leadership) within complex networks of meaning and power. Another aspect that makes *Group Psychology* important is the way in which it places object relations of the subject in a possible reading of spatial organization. This study contends that space is socially constructed and the social is spatially constructed.

Freud places the individual in her/his relation to her/himself and others, and this makes the placement social and spatial at the same time. Then group psychology probes the ways in which "the individual man as a member of a race, of a nation, of a caste, of a profession, of an institution, or as a component part of a crowd of people who have been organized into a group at some particular time for some definite purpose" (1921 4). Hence Freud distinguishes between the question of the individual alone from the question of the individual in a group in which a special instinct called the "social instinct" (herd instinct, group mind) directs behavior. His main question is to shed light into the workings of this social instinct through which individuals in the group submit to authority so deeply.

Freud discusses Gustave Le Bon's description of the group mind in his 1895 treaties of the subject in *The Crowd: A Study of the Popular Mind*, agreeing with Le Bon's description of the crowd as having contagious and hypnotic qualities where the individual cannot tolerate a delay between desire and fulfillment and somehow becomes primitive. There is a clear link between the group and "uncivilised" behavior, since the repression of unconscious desires is necessary for civilization: Freud writes that "in a group the individual is brought under conditions which allow him to throw off the repressions of his unconscious instinctual impulses" (1921 9) adding "when individuals come together in a group all their individual intentions fall away and all the cruel, brutal and destructive instincts, which lie dormant in individuals as relics of a primitive epoch, are stirred up to find gratification" (15). What keeps the group together is a special bond and this bond is characteristic of the group.

The bond comes with the "hypnotic," "charismatic," and "fanatical" leader to fulfill the group's need to obey and to believe in something, someone special even if this something or someone proves to be illusionary. After the killing of the father, his absence has become stronger, now the missing father (leader) is a central problem of authority in the group. The absent father, substituted by the leader enjoys unconditional submission from the individuals in the group where he is raised *above* the rest, displaying an example of a spatially constituted object relationship. Another spatial dimension for the group is that it is defined by a constitutive inside and a constitutive outside. As the wall in Kafka's tale "The Great Wall of China" while keeping the perceived "others" outside, also kept those encompassed by the wall in union, it is necessary for the group to demonize those who do not belong to the group. Therefore, to keep the common ideal the group needs an enemy. Thus the leader (person or ideal) has to be also aggressive to the "other" showing "hatred against a particular person or institution" (Freud, 1921: 41); this is equally effective for maintaining the integrity of the group.

For Freud the reason why individuals are willing to abandon their desire for independence is a part of the economy of the libido which is driven by the need to be loved. Then it is "love" that keeps the group together. This love is not something fixed, but it is complex, multiple and dynamic and it is so strong a feeling that individuals do not hesitate to abandon their freedom to act on their desires.

However this feeling of love is necessarily an illusion especially in hierarchical institutions like the military and religion where the union is achieved through a leader, an authority (commander in chief, God, Christ) in the form of a series of father-son relations. Therefore, in the army for example, there is a vertical *idealization* of the leader "a father who loves all soldiers equally" and a horizontal *identification* among the members who are "comrades among themselves" (Freud, 1921 34). Likewise in the church the group of believers are brothers through the equal love Christ has for them who is "their substitute father" (1921 33). While the strong bond of perceived "equal love" keeps the group together, it does so also by keeping outsiders, those who do not belong to the group, away in an intolerant and cruel manner: "a religion, even if it calls itself the religion of love, must be hard and unloving to those who do not belong to it" writes Freud (1921 39). This is not true only for the church, but structurally for every object relationship in which there is a common interest. Freud explains the workings of identification and idealization in the group through a visual representation and concludes "*A primary group of this kind is a number of individuals who have put one and the same object in the place of their ego ideal and have consequently identified themselves with one another in their ego*" (1921 61). Through idealization of the external object (the person her/himself, the leading person or idea, a person loved, or an object substituted for the loved one) ego ideal is formed; and members of the group are united by their relation to the external object besides their identification among themselves as equals before the illusion of love of the leader.

While the desires, conflicts, and needs of the individual in the group can be traced through her/his relationship to the external object, desires and conflicts within the urban space can be traced through its fabric, through the production of its specific space. In Manhattan urban space is immensely vertical with the skyscrapers' ever upward thrust. The main question then becomes if the vertical form is an ideal object through which New Yorkers (and Americans at large) are united? Can the skyscraper as an architectural product be a socially idealized object of American individualism? Does the skyscraper form offer a possible reading for its being an embodiment of an ego ideal?

These questions may provide an additional insight into the problem why New York has been insistent on growing vertically. The skyscraper form in its dominating presence in the urban fabric obviously has some effects on the psyche of the urban dweller. Since its creation during the end of nineteenth century, this dominating yet luring presence has been a locus of rendering the individual in the city for writers. The skyscraper fascinates the individual through its magnetic, grand and tall shape, and becomes an idealized external object. In this way it assumes a hypnotic role like that of the charismatic leader. At this point it is worth remembering that the leader does not have to be a person, it can very well be an object or an idea according to Freud. Koolhaas underlines the skyscraper's charismatic quality, its aura: "Building becomes Tower, landlocked lighthouse, ostensibly flashing its beams out to sea, but in fact luring the metropolitan audience to itself" (94).

In this object relationship the leader is spatially *above* the rest; those who are *under* its influence look *up* to it. French architect and urban planner Le Corbusier explains the fascination for the skyscraper in his *The Radiant City* (1964):

> In the age of speed, the skyscraper has petrified the city. The skyscraper has reestablished the pedestrian, him alone. [...] He moves anxiously near the bottom of the skyscraper, louse at the foot of the tower. The louse hoists himself up in the tower; it is night in the tower oppressed by the other towers: sadness, depression. [...] But on top of

those skyscrapers taller than the others, the louse becomes radiant. He sees the ocean and boats; he is above the other lice (133).

In line with the ego ideal, the distinctive skyscraper in its style, location, or tallness also outpours aggression in dwarfing anything that has contact with it. Like the horizontal wall in Kafka's story, this vertical form protects and keeps those who believe in (consciously or not) its display of power in union while alienating those who do not. Though this aggression is mainly towards the "other," insiders are not exempt from it. In the skyscraper's dwarfing influence, Le Corbusier's lice become O. Henry's insects.

O. Henry in his short story "Psyche and the Skyscraper" tells about the dehumanizing modern world set in New York through its central metaphor of the skyscraper. In a naturalist's world no one can escape victimization through all kinds of deterministic forces. In the story spatial determinism is revealed through the juxtaposition of the vertical (a downtown skyscraper) with the horizontal (the "smallest store in New York"). The story on the surface tells the love story of Daisy who is a nineteen year old "unphilosophical" girl working at a candy store, living in a little hall bedroom and her two suitors, Joe and Dabster. Joe is also "unphilosophical," he keeps the smallest store in New York which is "stuck like a swallow's nest against a corner of a downtown skyscraper" (113), and the pseudo-philosopher Dabster only "kidnaps" information from encyclopedias but does not have any real understanding or wisdom. Dabster is someone whom Freud would have called an "epistemophiliac" (s/he who suffers from an intense desire for knowledge) since the all desires are secretly libidinal, and are sublimated forms of sexual drive which is inseparable from the will to dominate and possess. "Your quarters are somewhat limited, Mr. –er—er, in comparison with the size of this building" (115) Dabster remarks in his attempt to get an upper hand for Daisy while Joe "of the Lilliputian emporium" has to fight against "steel" to win Daisy's heart.

To the philosopher from the top of the skyscraper people look like "irresponsible black waterbugs" that "crawl and circle and hustle about idiotically without aim or purpose" and all social distinctions dissolve; people from millionaires to "bootlacks" appear to be just "creeping, contemptible beetle[s]" (112).

The view from the top of the tower belittles all that lies below, but also de-differentiates or "massifies" them:

> From this high view the city itself becomes degraded to an unintelligible mass of distorted buildings and impossible perspectives; the revered ocean is a duck pond; the earth itself a lost golf ball. All the minutiae of life are gone. The philosopher gazes into the infinite heavens above him, and allows his soul to expand to the influence of his new view. He feels that he is the heir to Eternity and the child of Time. Space, too, should be his by the right of his immortal heritage, and he thrills at the thought that some day his kind shall traverse those mysterious aerial roads between planet and planet. The tiny world beneath his feet upon which this towering structure of steel rests as a speck of dust upon a Himalayan mountain—it is but one of a countless number of such whirling atoms. What are the ambitions, the achievements, the paltry conquests and loves of those restless black insects below compared with the serene and awful immensity of the universe that lies above and around their insignificant city? (112)

It is not the skyscraper, the "towering structure of steel" that is just as insignificant as a little speck of dust in universe, but it is the planet in universe that is the speck of dust as seen from the towering structure. On top of the skyscraper O. Henry's philosopher assumes that he rises above all other lice, taking his share in the power emanating from the tower. But the fact that the building creates a "dis-identification" with the mass requires a reworking of the models taken from Freud.

In Freud's analysis of the group psychology a horizontal identification among the members of the mass was necessary to their vertical idealization of the leader that was a substitute for the absent father. But in physically rising above the mass on the skyscraper, the philosopher is estranged from other fellow members. Identification does not work on the skyscraper in this spatially constituted relationship for the philosopher. Although on the skyscraper spatial dimension becomes one of constitutive above and constitutive below, it works differently for Daisy and Dabster. Dabster becomes disengaged from the ones below, not much as demonizing them but necessarily belittling them as mere insects. Without the small black spots moving aimlessly down the street, the philosopher on the top would not have been raised above. Therefore, Dabster has to be aggressive to the "others" below. Because he has failed to identify himself with the others, he puts his own ego narcissistically in place of his ego ideal. His ideal is himself again, as displayed by his reliance on his "encyclopedic" knowledge of the workings of the universe however empty. On the contrary Daisy's reaction will show that she identifies with the mass.

The "philosopher" Dabster takes Daisy to the observation deck of the skyscraper, Daisy's reaction is not like the philosopher's. When he explains that those little black spots moving down on the street are "bipeds" and "mere crawling insects going to and fro at random" (115), Daisy not liking her uprooting confronts Dabster suddenly saying "Oh, they ain't anything of the kind – they are folks!" (115) As one of the folk, Daisy completely identifies with the mass and eventually chooses Joe, the one who is also from the mass. She reacts to Dabster's scientific musings on a growing scale: first she says she does not like it in there, then feels threatened by height and declares she is afraid up there, shouts at Dabster angrily stamping her foot in a display of how decisive she is in wanting to go down, screams and cries out vehemently this time becoming wild-eyed. All this time Dabster keeps on talking "with his memory instead of his heart" (116) smiling "fatuously."

By the end of the story Daisy rushes out of the revolving door of the skyscraper to "Joe's funny little store tacked like a soap box to the corner of that great building" (114). Revolving doors -as opposed to the doors that simply open and close- rotate indiscriminately, spinning the contents of their implied threshold of the interior and the exterior. This architectural ambivalence mirrors the disintegration of Daisy's ego, made evident in her fear of height. Having been threatened by great height she runs to her epiphany as she tells Joe why she has chosen him: "Oh, Joe, I've been up on the skyscraper. Ain't it cozy and warm and homelike in here! I'm ready for you, Joe, whenever you want me" (117).

Indeed, the skyscraper form in its great height is "unhomely," but not uncanny (unheimlich) in Freud's terms in the story. The idea of homelike, that which belongs to a house and home reveals a sentiment of security and freedom from fear. However, as Freud writes in "The 'Uncanny'" (1919) the German word homelike or "heimlich" describes two contraries at the extreme ends of a series of qualities: "on the one hand it means what is familiar and agreeable, and on the other, what is concealed and kept out of sight" (933). Thus what is "canny" becomes "uncanny" and "the uncanny is that class of the frightening which leads back to what is known of old and long familiar" (930). Therefore, the uncanny is not something new but something which has become alienated from the mind through the process of repression: "the uncanny is something which is secretly familiar, which has undergone repression and then returned from it" (947). Freud links the uncanny to the death drive, to fear of castration, to the impossible desire to return to the womb, and "the uncanny has been interpreted as a dominant constituent of modern nostalgia, with a corresponding spatiality that touches all aspects of social life" (Vidler 10). Because in the story the skyscraper is not homelike, it cannot be a *locus suspectus*, an uncanny place; a phallic antithesis to the womb where all human beings belong. Vidler equates the uncanny not with the *modern* but with modern *nostalgia*. The skyscraper is also a substitute for that point of nostalgia, which is ultimately, the mother's womb for Freud that is cozy, warm and homelike.

But the skyscraper is also a "catalyst of consciousness" as Koolhaas argues: "In 50 years the Tower has accumulated the meanings of: catalyst of consciousness, symbol of technological progress, marker of pleasure zones, subversive short-circuiter of convention and finally self-contained universe" (93). Insofar as skyscrapers as architectural devices provoke self-consciousness, offering a bird's eye inspection of a common domain that can trigger a sudden spurt of collective energy and ambition (Koolhaas 33), the very same self-consciousness is another name for the self-observant and necessarily self-critical agent superego. It is the very place that Daisy has her epiphany, as does F. Scott Fitzgerald.

Inspections from above the skyscraper are a recurrent theme under "Manhattanism" through which the spatial self-consciousness they generate can be observed. Fitzgerald writes about his epiphany on the roof of the Empire State mediating on 1929 when the Great Depression hit the country in "My Lost City":

> From the ruins, lonely and inexplicable as the sphinx rose the Empire State Building and, just as it had been a tradition of mine to climb to the Plaza Roof to take leave of the beautiful city, extending as far as eyes could reach, so now I went to the roof of the last and most magnificent of towers. Then I understood—everything was explained: I had discovered the crowning error of the city, its Pandora's box. Full of vaunting pride the New Yorker had climbed here and seen with dismay what he had never suspected, that the city was not the endless succession of canyons that he had supposed but that *it had limits*—from the tallest structure he saw for the first time that it faded out into the country on all sides, into an expanse of green and blue that alone was limitless. And with the awful realization that New York was a city after all and not a universe, the whole shining edifice that he had reared in his imagination came crashing to the ground. That was the rash gift of Alfred E. Smith to the citizens of New York" (610).

The Empire State building is still a magnet for a "full" view of the city with its never ending waiting lines. On top of the Empire State one gets the feeling that this is not only a view of a city but a view of the so-called American empire. The physical condition of being elevated from others (other people, other cities, other countries) adds up to a feeling of shared power of the "empire." Taking its name from New York State's nickname, Empire State could only be grand in its form. Built in the 1930s when the depression hit the country hard the building was struggling to find lessees and was eventually dubbed "the empty state." However, it was (and still is) a civic icon for those who fought for survival in the streets because it was a radiant signifier, a symbol of hope for the economic strength of the nation. This is one of the reasons why the skyscrapers are often referred to as totems of capitalism. From Freud's account in *Totem and Taboo*, it is known that the totem occupies a significant role as a surrogate for the absent father. As totemic icons uniting the group, skyscrapers then point to an "absence," a "lack" in Lacanian terms.

2.2. The Lacanian Subject and the Built Environment

Lacan writes in "The Function of Speech and Language in Psychoanalysis" (1953): "Whether it wishes to be an agent of healing, training, or sounding the depths, psychoanalysis has but one medium: the patient's speech" (40). Then a psychoanalytic rendering of the city has to look for the city's voice. This voice emanates from the city's "gaze," its built environment defining the ways in which the city has been developed by its citizens. In a contingent web of discourses that the city comes "to speak," architecture necessarily points to multiple levels of signification. However, in Manhattan the overwhelming dominance of skyscrapers immediately known to everybody puts their verticality and monumentality, and ultimately the attendant power relations to foreground. Lefebvre's analysis in *The Production of Space* that draws on psychoanalysis clarifies the point:

> Altitude and verticality are often invested with a special significance, and sometimes even with an absolute one (knowledge, authority, duty), but such meanings vary from one society or 'culture' to the next. By and large, however, horizontal space symbolizes submission, vertical space power, and subterranean space death (236).

Therefore, a psychoanalytic frame that discusses the ways in which object relations signify power relations in space needs to lend both ears to the skyscrapers of New York.

The skyscraper in its vertical, erect form is like a "phallus" that everyone, men and women necessarily lack, yet never cease to try to have, or try to be according to Lacan. There is a constitutive abysmal lack at the centre of the Lacanian subject. Though Freud does not use the term phallus as something other than the penis, for Lacan it is an important concept that emphasizes the distinction between the male genital organ in its biological reality and the role that the same organ plays in fantasy in its symbolic functions (Evans 140).

Lacan writes in "The Signification of the Phallus" (1958) that the phallus can be better understood on the basis of its function: "In Freudian doctrine, the phallus is not a fantasy, if we are to view fantasy as an imaginary effect. Nor is it as such an object (part-, internal, good, bad, etc.) inasmuch as 'object' tends to gauge the reality involved in a relationship. Still less is it the organ – penis or clitoris- that it symbolizes" (275). Therefore, all subjects must assume a relationship to the phallus at the same time as they are inscribed differentially within the symbolic. The phallus makes sense as the single marker of sexual difference for Lacan since he argues that "a relation between the subject and the phallus [f]orms without regard to the anatomical difference of the sexes" (272). Further he adds that the phallus is necessarily a signifier: "[the phallus] is the signifier that is destined to designate meaning effects as a whole, insofar as the signifier conditions them by its presence as signifier" (275).

Lacan contends that the phallus is central in the Oedipus complex forming one of the three elements (the mother, the child, and the phallus) in the imaginary triangle that constitutes the pre-oedipal phase. The phallus is an imaginary object that goes to and fro between the mother and the child. The mother desires this object and the child looks for ways to satisfy the mother's desire by identifying with the phallus or with the phallic mother. Desire is only another term for lack, for something that is absent. However the Father intervenes, making it impossible for the child to identify with the imaginary phallus; thus "castrates" the child. Significantly it is castration that regulates desire. The child faces the Name-of-the-Father, symbolic father as a figure of the law, like Freud's prohibitive primal father; the superego. Terry Eagleton in his *Ideology: An Introduction* (1991) underlines the link between the Freudian superego and Lacanian Name-of-the-Father in their aggressive and threatening quality forming inescapable power relations:

> In the formation of the superego or Name-of-the-Father, power comes to entwine itself with the roots of the unconscious, tapping something of its awesome, implacable energy and directing this force sadistically against the ego itself. If political power is as recalcitrant as it is, then it is partly because the subject has come to love and desire the very law

which subjugates it, in the erotic perversion known as masochism (180).

Eagleton holds that this unconscious submission to authority is "one secret of the tenacity of political domination" (180) since the underprivileged classes through their narcissistic idealization of the leader see in the leader their own ideals, a place where they themselves want to be, reasoning under the influence of the ego ideal or the superego. In this mechanism the authority figure or the symbolic father works with all kinds of aggression and threat forcing the subject to internalize the law if s/he does not want to be cast out (castrated) in the society.

Symbolic father signifies the oedipal prohibition, saying "no" to any transgressive desire. Lacan points that the true function of the Father is "fundamentally to unite (and not to oppose) a desire to the Law" (1960 309). In the Oedipus complex the child can either accept the castration (the "no") seeing the threat as real accepting that he cannot be the mother's phallus or reject the prohibition. Man can only claim a symbolic phallus on the condition that he has accepted his own castration, that he has given up being the imaginary phallus, and by assuming that the woman's lack of the symbolic phallus is also a kind of possession (Evans 141). For Lacan lack is always related to desire whereby dialectic of power relations are made manifest. Then one can speak of a phallic power in object relations. Lefebvre underlines the point in relation to the phallic function of the space:

> The phallus is seen. The female genital organ, representing the world, remains hidden. The prestigious Phallus, symbol of power and fecundity, forces its way into view by becoming erect. In the space to come, where the eye would usurp so many privileges, it would fall to the Phallus to receive or produce them. The eye in question would be that of God, that of the Father or that of the Leader. A space in which this eye laid hold of whatever served its purposes would also be a space of force, of violence, of power restrained by nothing but the limitations of its means (262).

Lefebvre emphasizes the role of sight, or more properly the role of *gaze* in his assessment of the phallic space, hence leading the way to the relation between seeing, power relations and the skyscraper through a Lacanian reading. However, before probing into the "ways of seeing" the skyscraper, the constitutive dialectic of the image and the self in Lacanian terms should be posited.

The relation between the "I" and the "eye" can be traced back to the infantile psyche when the child is six to eighteen months old. In "The Mirror Stage as Formative of the *I* Function" (1949) Lacan significantly talks about the question of "the signification of space" (5) as the human child gets to recognize her/his own image in a mirror. During the encounter between the child and her/his image in the mirror, the child learns to distinguish between her/his own physical body and the empty reflection of that body in the mirror. The child gets to realize that her/his own movements are reflected from the image and are set within the mirror's reflection of the surrounding space. It is during this period that s/he acquires a "paranoiac knowledge" that signifies a real (her/his own body) and an illusionary existence (her/his image in the mirror) with other people and objects that form her/his immediate surroundings. This activity writes Lacan "reveals both a libidinal dynamism [...] and an ontological structure of the human world that fits in with my reflections on paranoiac knowledge" (1949 4). The presence of "the other" both in the external objects and in the subject's own body as reflected in the mirror makes it a paranoiac experience and further it makes all human thought essentially paranoiac in this sense.

In this context the mirror stage is an *identification* whereby the child experiences a transformation that shows her/his body as an image (imago) and assumes the instantaneous view of the image which refers to the fact that this is a "misrecognition" (1949 4). Significantly, for Lacan this identification with the image "manifests in an exemplary situation the symbolic matrix in which the *I* is precipitated in a primordial form, prior to being objectified in the dialectic of identification with the other, and before language restores to it, in the universal, its function as subject" (1949 4). This is exemplary since the child will function as a subject based on this identification that occurs through the eye and the *I*. This relationship is essentially spatial and visual and the form of the mirror stage is also "the rootstock of secondary identifications" (4) where it could be called the "ideal-I." The image in the mirror is a sort of Freud's ego ideal. However, Lacan does not explicitly state the ways in which identification with the image has been carried out except that this involves dialectical interaction. More important is the fact that, for Lacan, the form of the mirror stage:

> situates the agency known as the ego, prior to its social determination, in a fictional direction that will forever remain irreducible for any single individual or, rather, that will only asymptotically approach the subject's becoming, no matter how successful the dialectical syntheses by which he must resolve, as *I*, his discordance with his own reality (1949 4).

The reflection in the mirror provides an image of the child and her/his surrounding "exterior" to her/him, and this exteriority is placed in a space between the visible and the invisible. This fictional direction is constitutive of the formation of the "I" according to Lacan: "The total form of his body, by which the subject anticipates the maturation of his power in a mirage, is given to him only as a gestalt, that is, in an exteriority in which, to be sure, it appears to him as the contour of his stature that freezes it and in a symmetry that reverses it" (1949 4). Through the mirror the child is situated in space with the "derealizing effect of an obsession with space" (1949 5) therefore instituting a paranoiac existence about spatial relationships. The interacting worlds of the mirage (specular image) and the physical underlines the complexity of the dialectic between the child's partial perception of her/his own body since s/he can only see a part of her/his body in the mirror from a single perspective; s/he does not have a complete sight of her/his body. If s/he turns to see her/his back, s/he loses sight of her/his frontal image hence experiencing a "primordial Discord" (6). For Lacan the "fragmented body" is central to the mirror stage:

> The development is experienced as a temporal dialectic that decisively projects the individual's formation into history: the mirror stage is a drama whose internal pressure pushes precipitously from insufficiency to anticipation—and, for the subject caught up in the lure of spatial

identification, turns out fantasies that proceed from a fragmented image of the body to what I will call an 'orthopedic' form of its totality—and to the finally donned armor of an alienating identity that will mark his entire mental development with its rigid structure (1949 6).

Therefore the child is already alienated before her/his entry into the symbolic or the social carrying along the implication that the fictional characteristic of the specular image with which the child identifies is an act of "meconnaissance" or "misrecognition." The function of misrecognition characterizes the ego in all the defensive structures, most explicitly in negation (1949 8). In the child's looking at her/his own image in the mirror an obvious relationship between narcissistic libido and the alienating *I* function manifests itself with an attendant aggressiveness that will show itself in all relations with others from then on (1949 8), hence "the specular *I* turns into the social *I*" (1949 7).

Lacan's understanding of the formative mirror stage is essentially organized around a visual structure in which the child's relationship within and to herself/himself, within the world s/he was born into is a misrecognition of the spatial order of what s/he "sees," or more properly what s/he fails to "see." Significantly, the child sees (or fails to see since what s/he sees is illusory), "understands" the anatomical difference between the sexes visually —having or lacking the penis. The mirror stage is often referred to as a metaphor for the ways in which the child sees herself/himself in the reactions or in the "eyes" of others. However in its primacy of the visual that the dialectical object relations situate the child in a threshold between the look and the reflection it is important for the purposes of process of "seeing" the built environment and the subject. Therefore one can argue that there is a space not only between the subject and others but also in the subject. In any case this space is one of split and lack. The split between the specular image and "the constituting presence of the subject's gaze" formed by the castration anxiety explains the centrality of the phallus in the visual realm.

For Lacan there is a split between the organic eye and the gaze. He argues in "Of the Gaze as *Objet Petit a*" in *The Four Fundamental Concepts of Psychoanalysis* (1973) that the gaze comes before its eyes: "eye is only the metaphor of something I would prefer to call the seer's 'shoot' (*pousse*)–something prior to his eye. What we have to circumscribe [...] is the pre-existence of a gaze—I see only from one point, but in my existence I am looked at from all sides" (72-73). Although the eye has an organic existence, it cannot see itself directly. The split between the organic eye and the gaze does not manifest itself in the realm of the visible and the invisible for Lacan:

> [i]t is not between the invisible and visible that we have to pass. The split that concerns us is not the distance that derives from the fact that there are forms imposed by the world towards which the intentionality of phenomenological experience directs us—hence the limits we encounter in the experience of the visible. The gaze is presented to us only in the form of a strange contingency, symbolic of what we find on the horizon, as the thrust of our experience, namely, the lack that constitutes castration anxiety (1973 72-73).

The gaze underlines the link between the "little other" (*objet petit a*) as any imaginary object of desire which sets the desire in motion and the real, and this link can form an anxiety in the subject. "It is here that I propose that the interest the subject takes in his own split is bound up with that which determines it—namely, a privileged object, which has emerged from some primal separation, from some self-mutilation induced by the very approach of the real, who, in our algebra, is the *objet a*" (Lacan, 1973 84). Although *objet a* is seen only subjectively it "determines" all subjects "in the scopic relation," and the gaze is also in the field of the big Other: "The gaze sees itself... The gaze I encounter [...] is, not a seen gaze, but a gaze imagined by me in the field of the Other" (1973 84). The narcissistic association between the eye and *objet petit a* is a result of the castration anxiety which is formed on the subject's horizon by its gaze. However the subject's visual desire is not the desiring gaze of the "big Other". The gaze does not belong to the subject or the Other, but to the split between the two. Whereas the little other (a) is an illusory other being a reflection and projection of the ego in the imaginary order, the big Other (A) transcends the illusory otherness of the imaginary since it cannot be assimilated through identification. The Other designates radical alterity which Lacan equates with language and the law, placing it in the symbolic order (Evans

132-133). After setting the distinction between the eye and the gaze Lacan introduces "the stain," a function that allows eyes to apprehend the gaze:

> There is no need for us to refer to some supposition of the existence of a universal seer. If the function of the stain is recognized in its autonomy and identified with that of the gaze, we can see its track, its thread, its trace, at every stage of the constitution of the world, in the scopic field. We will then realize that the function of the stain and of the gaze is both which governs the gaze most secretly and that which always escapes from the grasp of that form of vision that is satisfied with itself in imagining itself as consciousness (1973 74).

Cannot be seen by the organic eye, the stain and the gaze interact, they exchange looks. Slavoj Žižek in *Looking Awry* (1991) introduces the gaze as marking the point in the object (in the picture) from which the subject viewing it is already gazed at; that is, the object gazes back at the subject (125). This is why the gaze functions as a stain, a spot in the picture disturbing the picture's transparent visibility and introducing an irreducible split in the subject's relation to the picture far from assuring the self-presence of the subject and her/his vision: the subject can never see the picture at the point from which it is gazing at the subject (Žižek 125). This "split between gaze and vision" writes Lacan is what forms the "scopic drive" (78).

The desire to look or the scopic drive is one of the four partial drives that Lacan identifies in his understanding of the drives. The oral, the anal, the scopic and the invocatory drives are essentially partial since they are only the aspects in which desire is manifested partly. The desire to look and comprehend the visible aspect of one's surroundings sound boundless and it is primary among the other three drives that it posits a centrality in the human's five senses. People perceive the world first through their visual sense, and it is indeed the key to the rest. Although the gaze has primacy over the organic eye, it nevertheless remains linked to it by light. Lacan suggests that in the subject "a quite different eye" apprehends more than just electromagnetic energy (1973 89) casting its own light. Though the eye casts its own light the split between the eye and its gaze is not formed only by light, it is outside; the subject is a picture that is being looked at: "What determines me [...] in the visible, is the gaze that is outside. It is through the gaze that I enter light and it is from the gaze that I receive its effects. Hence it comes about that the gaze is the instrument through which light is embodied and through which [...] I am *photographed*" (1973 106).

The eye is also under the surveillance of the scopic drive putting the subject into contact with the Other though barred. "The true function of the organ of the eye, the eye filled with voracity, [is] the evil eye" Lacan observes adding "It is striking when one thinks of the universality of the function of the evil eye, that there is no trace anywhere of a good eye of an eye that blesses" (1973 115). Moreover, the eye carries with it "the fatal function of being in itself endowed with a power to separate" which transgresses distinct vision (115). This power to "separate" carries out the act of gazing/looking and results in the ability to cut. The gaze functions on the side of the object and is capable of having real effects on the material world on the other hand the eye is on the side of the subject: "[i]n the scopic field, the gaze is outside, I am looked at, that is to say, I am a picture" (106). Lacan underlines subjective character of the eye: "Light may travel in a straight line, but it is refracted, diffused, it floods, it fills-the eye is a sort of bowl—it flows over, too, it necessitates, around the ocular bowl, a whole series of organs, mechanisms, defenses" (1973 94). It is the flowing over, excessive quality that pushes Lacan to formulate it as a drive. Therefore he opposes to the biologic rendering of the eye:

> We must now pose the question as to the exact status of the eye as organ. The function, it is said, creates the organ. This is quite absurd—function does not even explain the organ. Whatever appears in the organism as an organ is always presented with a large multiplicity of functions. In the eye, it is clear that various functions come together. [...] You will be able to see it if you fix your eye to one side (1973 101-102).

It is the fusion of the multiple functions that constitute the scopic drive as an element that goes beyond organic function taking together the various functions of eyes, the gaze, and necessarily the split between them. To see one needs something transparent, while to look is to search (to look for). Although Lacan points out that there is no evidence for an eye that blesses, something in opposition to the universal evil eye, there is a distinction between the eye as object (organ) and a subjective embodiment of the eye in its look. Moreover, the subject does not have to "blindly" submit to the invisible eye of a universal all-seeing power if s/he can learn to fix her/his eye to one side, to look "awry." In opposition to the dualist model of vision (seer/seen; subject/object, active/passive) Lacan puts forward an interacting three part model of the gaze in the relation between the subject, the object, and the Other. The seer/seen duality of the gaze dissolves and the world around the subject, the built environment looks at the subject as well. The "I" challenges the "eye."

Further, for Lacan the "screen" is one of the most common examples of the split between the eye and the gaze. As the gaze shows, so does the screen but only in masking. Screen focuses the imaginary characteristics of the gaze for the subject in a discreet manner. Although Lacan points to an essential difference between painting and representation in his analysis of the gaze, architecture as representation functions like a picture. Insofar as "architecture privileges sight" and "mobilizes the desire to look" (Nalbantoğlu 58) the scopic drive sheds light on the diffuse power relations in the urban fabric. The subject is not the only one that is driven by the urge to look, but the architectural product also "looks back" through the gaze. Because the space, the built environment is not fixed, but is dynamic in a dialectical relationship with the subject, it shows and hides, protects and threatens, unites and separates, and provides ways of understanding the interaction between space, identity and power. Since the task of psychoanalysis according to Lacan is to "lay bare aggressiveness" (1949 9) skyscrapers are perfect spatial examples for that task. Specifically, distinctive skyscrapers with their tall erectility in the urban fabric cannot escape the visual field thereby mediating power in their phallic form as Lefebvre argues:

> The arrogant verticality of skyscrapers, and especially of public and state buildings, introduces a phallic or more precisely a phallocratic element into the visual realm; the purpose of this display, of this need to impress, is to convey an impression of authority to each spectator.

Verticality and great height have ever been the spatial expression of potentially violent power" (98).

The verticality and political arrogance of towers, or their feudalism as Lefebvre puts it, already implies a future alliance between the ego and phallus unconsciously, and all the more effectively for that (262). Lefebvre argues that the monumental vertical built form is phallic: "Metaphorically it symbolizes force, male fertility, masculine violence [...] Phallic erectility bestows a special status on the perpendicular (287). Under the surveillance of the gaze on the side of the object, the subject disappears —something that Lacan defines as *aphanisis*- in the process of alienation. Disappearance institutes the dialectic of desire in the fundamental division of the subject, and the subject in the social space is ultimately under prohibition:

> That space signifies is incontestable. But what it signifies is dos and don'ts — and this brings us back to power. Power's message is invariably confused — deliberately so; dissimulation is necessarily part of any message from power. Thus, space indeed 'speaks' – but it does not tell all. Above all, it prohibits" (Lefebvre 142).

Then, one can see that the dialectic between power relations and space is one of prohibition and illusion. Like Lacan, Lefebvre argues that there is a split between the eye and the gaze. The organic eye discerns the objects while the gaze is associated with detachment. The image institutes a gap (like Lacan's "lack") between the body and space thereby engendering a free-flowing desire, a desire that has no object. The mirror constitutes one of the many alienations of the subject since it splits the body through the eye and its specular image, enforcing boundaries between the subject and its others (Lefebvre 201-202). For Lefebvre these boundaries are made manifest through the gaze and the phallus in manifesting power relations in space (204). The phallus is central to Lefebvre's argument of monumentality in that the social space of capitalist relations is characterized by some masked, symbolic power:

> Monumentality, for instance, always embodies and imposes a clearly intelligible message. It says what it wishes to say – yet it hides a good deal more: being political, military, and ultimately fascist in character,

monumental buildings mask the will to power and the arbitrariness of power beneath signs and surfaces which claim to express collective will and collective thought (143).

Skyscrapers are phallic because they are "erect," super tall and associated with power and wealth. It is in the skyscraper's phallic form and its being a "civic monument" to the ideal of individualism of the nation that its immense, yet hidden power emanates. Accordingly Lefebvre states: "monuments have a phallic aspect, *towers* exude arrogance, and the bureaucratic and political authoritarianism immanent to a repressive space is everywhere" (149) [emphasis mine]. Insofar as a skyscraper assumes distinction in its location, style, and great height, that is insofar as it is a landmark in the urban fabric, it controls the subject's perception of spatial significations and more importantly created and maintained by the big money, it reproduces the value systems of the powerful. As all buildings are marked by the production of spaces of domination, the skyscraper disguised as a civic monument condenses the diffuse power relations into a particular site. Although monumental buildings hide, legitimize or help subjects internalize power relations, they say what they want to say clearly, making the quality of that space closed to alternative readings, and by doing so, they ultimately draw the subjects into an illusion that the values they represent are common and shared among the society. Spaces are never empty, and the content for monumental space is "designed to conceal: namely, the phallic realm of (supposed) virility. It is at the same time a repressive space: nothing in it escapes the surveillance of power" (Lefebvre 147). Although Lefebvre does not allude to Lacan, it is clear in this passage that he makes use of two central Lacanian concepts: the phallus and the gaze.

From this point, skyscrapers as monumental buildings function like the phallus since they make visible and "look back" to the subject in the street, reproducing repressive spaces which both celebrate entrepreneurship and individualism while unleashing their aggressiveness, threatening to castrate (cast out) the ones who are doubtful of the celebration. In this space body is fragmented into images, desire is shattered, and "life explodes into a thousand pieces" (Lefebvre 309). This violently castrating space "isolates the phallus, projecting it into a realm outside the body, then fixes it in space (verticality) and brings it under the surveillance of the eye [...] because of the process of localization, because of the fragmentation and specialization of space" (Lefebvre 310). This is a site of disintegration, dissolution, and alienation for the subject.

This type of oppressive vertical space is clearly observed in John Dos Passos's *Manhattan Transfer* (1925). Dos Passos's Manhattan is a locus of loss, an urban space deeply fragmented as underlined by the novel's fragmented characters and text. The fragmented narrative of the novel juxtaposes desperate and searching characters with the towering skyscrapers, enabling the transfer of the characters' perplexed emotions into the built environment while the built environment help shape these emotions.

During the 1920s, when Dos Passos was writing *Manhattan Transfer*, skyscrapers had already come into maturity as monuments of corporate power serving functional and symbolic ends. By the mid 20s the symbolic element (display of power and prestige) in the skyscraper form began to surpass the functional. The booming economy of the "Jazz Age" was coming to an end, eventually to be cut down by the stock exchange crash of 1929, but the skyscrapers were going up even taller though not enough lessees could be found to rent the offices in the skyscrapers to compensate for the investment in the buildings. Nevertheless, skyscrapers were growing taller this time perhaps serving something psychological:

> The skyscraper arose in answer to the desire of the herd to become a super-herd; to the ambition of the sport cards to become face cards. Skyscrapers appear always and only on those sacred areas which for some reason have become the blue heaven of the business man. High buildings in preferred areas owe their existence to the same cause as high prices for front-row seats at a show (Stern 589).

Lewis Mumford argues that American architecture in the late 20s was getting rid of the imitation of the past forms: "between 1924 and 1928 it seemed that American architecture had at last emerged from its feeble, romantic, pseudo-historic posturing, and was creating something that, however harsh and dehumanized, represented what was vital and effective in our civilization" (quoted in Stern 589). The new American architecture was fusing the economic and materialist aspirations of the investors and architects alike with a new independence form past architectural examples and it found this new language in the skyscraper form. The growing dominance of the skyscraper in New York coincides with the economic speculation of the 20s and it is the same dominance that underlines the urban symbolism in *Manhattan Transfer*.

Dos Passos, like many other modernists, saw an enchanting chaos in New York which he masterfully depicted in the novel. He writes to a friend in a letter in 1920:

> New York –after all-is magnificent, a city of cavedwellers, with a frightful, brutal ugliness about it, full of thunderous voices of metal grinding on metal and of an eternal sound of wheels which turn, turn on heavy stones. People swarm meekly like ants along designated routes, crushed by the disdainful and pitiless things among them (quoted in Ludington 200).

In the same letter Dos Passos also evokes the towering and corrupt Biblical cities which he would employ in the novel:

> Nineveh and Babylon, of Ur of the Chaldees, of the immense cities which loom like basilisks behind the horizon in ancient Jewish tales. Where the temples rose as high as mountains and people ran trembling through dirty little alleys to the constant noise of whips with hilts of gold. O for the sound of a brazen trumpet which, like the voice of the Baptist in the desert, will sing again about the immensity of man in this nothingness of iron, steel, marble, and rock. Night time especially is both marvelous and appalling, seen from the height of a Roof Garden, where women with raucous voices dance in an amber light, the bluegray bulk of the city cut up by the enormous arabesques of electric billboards, when the streets where automobiles scurry about like cockroaches are lost in a golden dust, and when a pathetic little moon, pale

and dazzled, looks at you across a leaden sky (quoted in Ludington 200-201).

Dos Passos's comparison is highly interesting since he was not a fan of religion who found the Bible to a "disagreeable" book, "if devilishly well written, for the most part" (quoted in Ludinton 231). Also, Ludington rightfully argues that "a critic could not ask for a better statement of what Dos Passos intended to portray in *Manhattan Transfer*" (201). Indeed, Old Testament allusions abound in the novel in chapter titles such as "One More River to Jordan," "Rejoicing City That Dwelt Carelessly," and "The Burthen of Nineveh;" and in many chapter head notes and narrative segments New York City is associated with the corrupt Biblical cities such as Sodom, Babylon and Nineveh which are marked for destruction, revealing an apocalyptic tone (Vanderwerken 253). Accordingly, in the novel Stan contemplates: "Who am I? Where am I? City of New York, State of New York ... Stanwood Emery age twentytwo occupation student ..." (228) [ellipses in original] and sitting in Battery Park, a focal neighborhood for downtown skyscrapers, associates the ruined Biblical cities that are corrupted by their own wealth and success, and other old vertical cities with New York:

> There *was* Babylon and Nineveh; they *were* built of brick. Athens *was* gold marble columns. Rome *was* held upon broad arches of rubble. In Constantinople the minarets flame like great candles round the Golden Horn ... O there's one more river to cross. Steel, glass, tile, concrete will be the materials of the skyscrapers. Crammed on the narrow island the millionwindowed buildings will jut, glittering pyramid on pyramid like the white cloudsheads above a thunderstorm ... (229) [ellipses in original; emphases mine]

In the passage, the incorporation of the skyscrapers of New York with Biblical cities posits architectural endeavor as a precursor to mass destruction. Babylon with its ruined tower, Nineveh with its corruption, Athens with its vertical columns, Rome with its arches, Constantinople or Istanbul with its towering minarets serve as backgrounds for the skyscraper filled New York. Rome and Constantinople, for example, were once the capitals of the most powerful empires of the world, but in 1925 there was no longer a Roman Empire, or an

Eastern Roman or an Ottoman Empire. Today Athens and Rome as de jure capitals, Istanbul as an economic and cultural capital are parts of struggling economies. At the time of the novel, Rome was the capital of Italy, one of the triumphant countries of the World War I only to be defeated in the following world war, and no longer enjoyed worldwide dominance. Istanbul was not the capital of the newly founded modern Turkish Republic that succeeded the Ottoman Empire, though remained as the spiritual capital like New York did for the United States. New York too *is* the economic and cultural capital of the "American Empire" that emerged as a superpower after World War II with its economic and political power embedded in its vertical fabric. The undertone of the association reminds the reader of Archibald MacLeish's poem entitled "You, Andrew Marvell" where the speaker laying face down under the noon sun in Illinois contemplates the westward course of the sun into darkness, casting shadows of death over once powerful ancient cities. The speaker and his country enjoy full flush of power and youth, but like the ruined ancient cities their time will come too. As individual time passes and comes to a close in death always hearing "time's winged chariot hurrying near" so do historical epochs. Further, as exemplified in New York, architectural hubris is not foreign to the society's decadence and deterioration.

Moreover, of all the Biblical cities invoked by Dos Passos, Babylon stands out with the centrality of the Tower of Babel. As was discussed before in "man's" attempt to build a tower that would reach unto heaven a collective vanity and pride, an attempt on part of the human to be gods onto themselves was punished by God. Before, people had spoken one language and were able to communicate, but God punished their vanity by confusing their language, thus terminating all connection among people. It is the confusion of their language, non-communication that brings an end to the tower. Significantly, the symbolic end that the skyscrapers have served was one of pride and vanity in that they rose like corporate banners in the sky "making names" for the businesses. Also the skyscrapers of the novel become modern "towers" of Babel since no communication and connection remains in the chaotic city.

The phallomorphic skyscrapers of the novel enhance the sense of oppression, fragmentation, alienation and dehumanization of the novel's setting, in a way that Mumford would call deflating the "social drama." "The novel's technique of fragmentation, of dislocation, of discontinuous narrative itself reflects not only a modern confusion of language but confusion in society at large" (Vanderwerken 254). Significantly, the fragmented narrative and the abundant use of ellipses mirror the fragmented modern urban society and the fragmented subjects in that society. A sense of loss unites the conflict and tension between the subject, the society and built environment. While the characters look at the skyscrapers, looking for meaning and identity in the urban despair; the skyscrapers look back at them with an oppressive "gaze" facilitating their lack of understanding.

In the most revealing passage for the dialectic of aggression, power, the built environment and the subject, by the end of the novel Jimmy Herf, the downwardly mobile journalist who is the chief interpreter of the city and the skyscraper, "loses faith in words," and his loss is mirrored in the skyscraper with which he seems to be obsessed:

> All these April nights combing the streets alone a skyscraper has obsessed him, a grooved building jutting up with *uncountable bright windows* falling unto him out of a scudding sky. Typewriters rain continual nickelplated confetti in his ears. [...] And he walks round blocks and blocks looking for the door of the humming tinselwindowed skyscraper, round blocks and blocks and still no door. Every time he closes his eyes the dream has hold of him, every time he stops arguing audibly with himself in pompous reasonable phrases the dream has hold of him. Young man to save your sanity you've got to do one of two things ... Please mister where's the door to this building? Round the block? Just round the block ... one of two unalienable alternatives: go away in a dirty soft shirt or stay in a clean Arrow collar. But what's the use of spending your whole life fleeing the City of Destruction? What about your unalienable right, Thirteen Provinces? His mind unreeling phrases, he walks on doggedly. There's nowhere in particular he wants to go. If only I still had faith in words (327) [ellipses in original; emphasis mine].

April does not provoke regeneration or hope for Jimmy in "The Waste Land" called New York, it is indeed "the cruelest month." The city has the power to reduce its dwellers into "hollow men" as Eliot would have it, in an immense urban despair. As a journalist, a man living on written words Jimmy's loss of faith in words further underlines his isolation. Jimmy, the only character who would escape from the "beautiful catastrophe," is Dos Passos's agent to interpret the city. In this nightmarish passage Jimmy's isolation, his inability to find the "door" is revealed against the physical description of Manhattan, bringing together a union of the physical built environment and the emotional response on part of the subject.

The novel's preoccupation with the transcendence of gaze is evident in its frequent return to agents of seeing and understanding such as windows and doors. The window is particularly important for Dos Passos because it is like a framed picture, and the door is a kind of aesthetic threshold that allows contemplation of the built environment. However, in Jimmy's inability to find the door and therefore an access to the skyscraper prevents him to be an insider of the skyscraper. He is left out in the open, he can only look at the skyscraper and endure the gaze back. In this the skyscraper represents a promise of success that is never delivered. The skyscraper is not homelike, characterized by its shining but blank windows. However, none of the characters in the novel (including Jimmy) look out from these windows. Instead, in the oppressive gaze of the skyscraper Jimmy imagines the Woolworth Building is looking at him, likening the uncanny gaze of the building to an architectural surveillance system and the author's all-seeing (omniscient) point of view at the same time:

> He stood beside a pile of pink newspapers on the curb, taking deep breaths, looking up the glistening shaft of the Woolworth [...] As he got away from it the Woolworth pulled out like a telescope. He walked north through the city of shiny windows, through the city of scrambled alphabets, through the city of gilt letter signs (228).

The "scrambled alphabets" and "gilt letter signs" suggest the ever growing aggression emanating from the city's skyscrapers. Jimmy's illusive freedom after he has just quit his job leads him to imagine himself as a "towering" omnipotent structure:

> He began to swell, felt himself stumbling big and vague, staggering like a pillar of smoke above the April streets, looking into the windows of machineshops, buttonfactories, tenementhouses, felt the grime of bedlinen and the smooth whir of lathes, wrote cusswords on typewriters between the stenographer's fingers, mixed up the pricetags in departmentstores [...] He dropped sickeningly fortyfour stories, crashed (229-230).

Jimmy's identification with the skyscraper echoes a much more explicit desire in Stan's words: "Kerist I wish I was a skyscraper" (230). Stan, contemplating suicide, identifies himself with a skyscraper, a tower of strength which he lacks and which is capable of surviving in the apocalyptic city. The skyscraper becomes an ego ideal for Jimmy and Stan, a substitute of the lost childhood narcissism lending a part of the ego to an external object. Their obsession or fascination with the skyscraper does not change the physical structure of the building but because it is idealized by Jimmy and Stan (the subject) they now want to *be* that object. Indeed the skyscraper as a totemic icon, a lost or absent father represents the very loss, a colossal lack in their existence. In the skyscraper's monumental verticality Jimmy and Stan want to have, or rather they want to be the phallus. No trace of life is seen in the skyscraper, it only has shiny windows. It is the empty imago of the mirror stage with which the child identifies. In that, through Jimmy and Stan's look and the gaze back from the skyscraper they falsely identify with the skyscraper, because the fictional characteristic of the specular image is an act of "méconnaissance." Significantly, as the mirror stage is often referred to as a metaphor for the ways in which the child sees herself/himself in the reactions or in the "eyes" of others, the primacy of the gaze of the skyscraper adds up to Jimmy's isolation, and it leads to Stan's suicide. The split, fragmentation, and self-destructive alienation in Jimmy and Stan are mirrored in their identification with the skyscraper underlining the dialectic of the relation between the subject and space: it becomes impossible to separate the subject (who s/he is) from space (where s/he is).

"The image of the Manhattan skyline may stand for vitality, power, decadence, mystery, congestion, greatness, or what you will, but in each case that sharp picture crystallizes and reinforces the meaning" (Lynch 8-9). These are all associated with phallic power towering on Manhattan's skyscrapers. Manhattan's skyscrapers with their phallic arrogance stand in opposition to the canyon like, dirty and congested streets below them and the people who inhabit those streets, looking up the skyscrapers. The destructive phallic power of the skyscraper and Jimmy's vision of himself as a skyscraper with its "drop" and "crash" not only echoes Stan's suicide, but also his own metaphorical death. Jimmy's metaphorical death is ultimately liberating since he is the only character who is allowed to leave "the city of destruction" hitting the open road penniless but hopeful. The fact that Dos Passos kills the aspiring architect Stan is a testament implying that the apocalyptic city gets the better of any potentially redemptive urban narrative. The skyscraper in its oppressive, yet hidden gaze of a sort of architectural surveillance system leads to an understanding of societies founded on discipline.

3. TOWER / POWER

> *Fear [i]s mediated.*
> Theodor Adorno, "Sociology and Psychology," 1967

> *[I]deological and political hegemony in any society depends on an ability to control the material context of personal and social experience. For this reason, the materializations and meanings given to money, time, and space have more than a little significance for the maintenance of political power.*
> David Harvey, *The Condition of Postmodernity*, 1990

Architecture underlines the point that the built environment is the product of ideological interests and is expressive of these ideological interests. The built environment one sees, lives in, and experiences is typically one reflecting the differential power of groups to build as they please. Further, architecture can also be understood as a means of controlling masses as Foucault's work has shown.

Power in relations between people involves control over others and it is the most generalized meaning of power. However, power as a term derives from the Latin *potere*, meaning "to be able," underlining the capacity to achieve some end, having the necessary means or skill or know-how or authority to do something, as in "being able to swim." Therefore, the distinction between power as capacity and power as control is fundamental to all that follows (Isaac 42). While power as capacity is able to liberate, power as control oppresses. Since it is the aim of this study to unfold the architectonic strategies at work in the silent but oppressive skyscrapers, the concept of power as control is taken to be its primary meaning, although it is difficult to separate these two meanings of power from a Foucaultian perspective. As French philosopher Paul Ricoeur says: "Power is one of the splendours of man that is eminently prone to evil" (255).

The built environment acts as a mediator of power. It mediates, constructs and reproduces power relations. However silent, architectural products control the individual in her/his dwelling places, as her/his action is both structured and shaped by walls, doors, and windows. "As a form of discourse, built form constructs and frames meanings. Places tell us stories; we read them as spatial text (Dovey 1). Architectural products, the built environment is necessarily shaped according to certain interests in quest of profit, status, power, or aesthetics. However, the built environment is taken as a given; it is taken for granted most of the time, and this unquestioned, silent nature is the very key to its complex relations with power.

Thus French social theorists Michel Foucault and Pierre Bourdieu's works offer indispensable insight into the reproductions of the relations of power in the built form. Because while Foucault argues that power in its micro practices operate through the normalizing gaze of surveillance regimes in that space constructs subjects by employing the built form as disciplinary technology, Bourdieu suggests that the built environment constructs the experience of the subject as spatial ideology in his concept of the *habitus*. Further, Bourdieu's theory of symbolic power and symbolic violence adds another explanatory dimension to the workings of the Lacanian and Foucaultian gaze on the subject.

Although Foucault and Bourdieu seem to have a certain distance to psychoanalysis, their works prove to be complementary to those of Freud and Lacan. What these two theorists have in common with psychoanalysis is their interest in the ways in which power relations work through the individual and society at large. This study contends that the relation between psychoanalysis and social theory is strong and complementary following Adorno:

> The separation of society and psyche is false consciousness; it perpetuates conceptually the split between the living subject and the objectivity that governs the subjects and yet derives from them. [...] While social laws cannot be 'extrapolated' from psychological findings, the individual is [...] simultaneously the agent of the social determinations that shape him (1967 69, 73)[4].

---

[4] Adorno's Marxist point in defining the link between psychology and sociology has to be disregarded to a large degree for the purposes of the study at hand, since no specific focus

For Foucault history has to be understood according to the discourses and *epistemes*[5] of the past; Freudian and Lacanian psychoanalysis take discourses of the unconscious workings of the mind to lay out the history of the subject. For Foucault it is through a "genealogical" analysis of the past that we gain some insight into the way in which the present has been produced; for Freud and Lacan it is through an analytical and structural analysis of the subject's past that one has some light into the ways in which the subject is produced.

Although Foucault sees psychoanalysis itself as a form of repression and as a micro-tactic of power most of the time, he is concerned with examining the past as a means of diagnosing the present, therefore he refers to psychoanalysis from time to time in that psychoanalysis probes the ways in which the self and the representation of the self through unconscious ways come into play. He writes in the last chapter of *The Order of Things* (1966):

> In setting itself the task of making the discourse of the unconscious speak through consciousness, psychoanalysis is advancing in the direction of that fundamental region in which the relations of representation and finitude come into play. Whereas all the human sciences advance towards the unconscious only with their back to it [...] psychoanalysis points directly to it [...] psychoanalysis moves towards the moment [...] This means that, unlike the human sciences, which, even while turning back towards the unconscious, always remain within the space of the representable, psychoanalysis advances and leaps over representation, overflows it on the side of finitude, and thus reveals, where one had expected functions bearing their norms, conflicts burdened with rules, and significations forming a system, the simple fact that it is possible for there to be system (therefore signification), rule (therefore conflict), norm (therefore function). And in this region representation remains in suspense (374).

---

has been allotted to class conflict in probing the ways in which power is mediated through the built environment.
[5] Broad changes, ruptures in intellectual outlook.

Further Foucault makes extensive use of psychoanalytic knowledge. A great deal of Foucault's work focus on the relationship between the gaze and seeing as the very first sentence of his *Birth of the Clinic* (1963) demonstrates: "This book is about space, about language, and about death; it is about the act of seeing, the gaze" (ix). Foucault and Lacan's work coincides on the relation of the organic eye and its gaze.

In his "A Preface to Transgression" (1963a) Foucault describes the split nature of the organic eye: "the eye, a small white globe that encloses it darkness, traces a limiting circle that only sight can cross. And the darkness within, the somber core of the eye, pours out into the world like a fountain that sees, that is, which lights up the world" (44-45). Although Foucault seems to be talking about an autonomous eye, a panoptical, all-seeing eye, there is something more primary to the autonomous sight of the eye:

> [t]he eye also gathers up all the light of the world in the iris, that small black spot, where it is transformed into the bright night of an image. The eye is mirror and lamp: it discharges its light into the world around it, while in a movement that is not necessarily contradictory, it precipitates this same light into the transparency of its well (1963a 45).

Here Foucault notes the blind spot, the role of the scotoma[6], in the location of the seer and the seen. It is this Lacanian split between the gaze and the eye that Foucault uses to define transgression. Once crossed, the limit contributes to the birth of something entirely new, but all the same related to the prior object.

The publication of *The Order of Things: An Archaeology of the Human Sciences* in 1966 brings Foucault into conflict with Lacan about the question of the psychological dimension of human perception. Foucault's archeology of knowledge begins with a poetic reading of Diego Velásquez's painting "Las Meninas" (1656) where he begins his theory of "man" and the question of modern subjectivity. Although Foucault's reading of "Las Meninas" displays a difference between his theory of the subject and the subject of psychoanalysis,

---

[6] The isolated area of diminished vision within the visual field.

"Las Meninas," his introductory chapter to *The Order of Things*, is also about the role of the image in the persistent place of the imaginary within the symbolic; both Lacanian terms.

As for Bourdieu, despite a serious degree of reservations initially, psychoanalysis always seems to have a place in his works. As Jean-François Fourny suggests, these initial reservations have evolved in time and psychoanalysis has played an increasingly important role in his works (103). Fourny also argues that psychoanalysis is also the symptom of Bourdieu's sociology, and these two disciplines are also closely linked (104). Bourdieu begins his seminal *Distinction: A Social Critique of the Judgement of Taste* (1979) putting forward the very link, and praising psychoanalysis: "Sociology is rarely more akin to social psychoanalysis than when it confronts an object like taste, one of the most vital stakes in the struggles fought in the field of the dominant class and the field of cultural production" (11).

However, Bourdieu has an ambiguous, a problematic stance towards psychoanalysis although he borrows certain concepts from it. For example in line with psychoanalysis, in *Outline of a Theory of Practice* (1972) he defines the unconscious as the forgetting of history which is produced by history itself, and asserts that individual history, even in its sexual dimension, is socially determined. Moreover, Bourdieu contends that sociology takes biology and psychology as a given, and attempts to establish how the social world uses, transforms, and transfigures them (Fourny 103-107).

By 1993, with the publication of *The Weight of the World: Social Suffering in Contemporary Society*, sociology and psychoanalysis become complementary disciplines as Bourdieu asserts that sociology does not intend to substitute its explanatory method for that of psychoanalysis; it only intends to construct in a different fashion certain facts that psychoanalysis takes up as objects of inquiry, fixing on aspects of reality that psychoanalysis dismisses as secondary or insignificant, or treats as screens to be traversed in order to reach the essential (608). Bourdieu assigns the task of analyzing "aspects of reality that psychoanalysis dismisses as secondary or insignificant" to sociology. In *The Masculine Domination* (1998), Bourdieu ventures onto the psychoanalytic territory in studying sexual difference and its anthropological bases. The book treats the Kabyle tradition as an objective archeology of the human unconscious, as the instrument of a true "socioanalysis" (19). It is a question here of a "historical" unconscious, resulting from an effort at historical construction (61). On the one hand, Bourdieu stresses that the constitution of the individual unconscious in Freud's works is related to "a generic and universal family structure," whereas, on the other hand, the social aspect of this constitution is not "truly excluded," and he ultimately concludes that the unconscious is at once collective and individual. Bourdieu admittedly takes precautions and expresses reservations, as when he asserts that "socioanalysis" historicizes the difference between the sexes rather than naturalizing it, as does psychoanalysis. Nonetheless, it is no longer psychoanalysis that serves as sociology's occasional auxiliary, as in Bourdieu's earlier works, but rather "socioanalysis," which seems to fall under the banner of psychoanalysis and its fundamental concepts (Foury 100-111).

3.1. Foucault and the Panopticon

> *Liberty is a practice [...] it can never be inherent in the structure of things to guarantee the exercise of freedom. The guarantee of freedom is freedom.*
> Michel Foucault, "Space, Power and Knowledge," 1984

Primarily the concept of power points to the exercise of force or control over individuals or particular social groups by other individuals or groups. In this view, power is taken as something not intrinsic to the constitution of either individuals or society. However, Foucault redefines power so that it exists not as something that is exercised over individuals or groups but as something constitutive of both the relations which exist between groups, making it equally constitutive of individual and group identity themselves. He argues that "power is neither given, nor exchanged, nor recovered, but rather exercised, and that it only exists in action. [...] Power is not primarily the maintenance and reproduction of economic relations, but is above all a relation of force" (1980 89). It is important for Foucault's analysis that power is not only constitutive of social reality and subjectivity, but it is also a reproduction of relational forces.

Foucault also underlines the ever shifting disguises of power: "power is tolerable only on condition that it masks a substantial part of itself. Its success is proportional to its ability to hide its own mechanisms" (1980 86). This masking of mechanisms of power relations is also a central theme for Bourdieu who calls this process as the workings of a "symbolic power." However, for Foucault, unfolding the mechanisms and effects of power does not rely on the analysis of power as repression.

Space is never empty, as Foucault observes in "Of Other Spaces: Utopias and Heterotopias," it is always "saturated with qualities" (349). Foucault's concern with space is mainly an interest that space mediates power. "If space, as Foucault would have it, is always a container of social power, then the reorganization of space is always a reorganization of the framework through which social power is expressed" (Harvey 255). As for the art of building in spaces, architecture for Foucault is

> only taken as an element of support, to ensure a certain allocation of people in space, a *canalization* of their circulation, as well as the coding of their reciprocal relations. So it is not only considered as an element in space, but is especially thought of as a plunge into a field of social relations in which it brings about some specific effects (1984 253).

Foucault discusses the specific effects architectural products help impose on subjects with the example of the panopticon in *Discipline and Punish* (1975). He also argues in *Discipline and Punish*, *Power/Knowledge* (1980) and elsewhere that a rupture in power relations has occurred since the eighteenth century when enlightenment and the parallel rise of scientific rationality, the nation-state, modern institutions, capitalism and industrial advances have occurred. Moreover, he says in "Space, Knowledge and Power:" "in the eighteenth century one sees the development of reflection upon architecture as a function of the aims and techniques of the government of societies" (239). For Foucault, the Enlightenment with its emphasis on knowledge and truth engenders new forms of domination disguising them as liberation. This is a new knowledge/power regime which requires that "we replace the notion of power as a relation of dominance of one person over another with a concept of power dispersed throughout the social body. Such power operates through social and spatial practices and is embedded in institutions" (Dovey 19). This is what Foucault calls "disciplinary power" since it operates through normalization and one of the qualities of power is that the norm creates ever anew shadowy spaces of abnormality or transgression on its periphery. It is also a "bio-power" because it acts on and through the body to produce docile subjects.

Disciplinary power transforms human beings into subjects through micro-practices. The most important of these micro-practices is the *gaze*. For Foucault, the gaze, which is at once the gaze of science and of the state (power/knowledge) is a practice of disciplinary control through asymmetrical visibility. Architectural practices here play an important role, and above all as Foucault argues, "Space is fundamental in any form of communal life; space is fundamental in any exercise of power" (1984 252). Within spatial relations a normalizing regime is established and the gaze of surveillance controls deviations from it.

Through Foucault's account of the growth of disciplinary institutions from the eighteenth century in *Discipline and Punish*, the spatial dimension in his understanding of power unfolds itself. By the end of the eighteenth and the beginning of the nineteenth centuries prisons turn their attention from spectacles of punishment like torturing criminals on a scaffold in a public space (public execution) so as to make people witnesses to the torture the criminal is subjected to, thus indirectly forcing them to avoid deviations from the law for themselves, to techniques of normalization and "cure." "The disappearance of torture as a public spectacle" (7) by which "the sovereign's surplus power was manifested" (202) gives way to the coercion of surveillance. It was during that time "a new 'economy' of power" was established, argues Foucault, "procedures which allowed the effects of power to circulate in a manner at once continuous, uninterrupted, adapted, and 'individualized' throughout the entire social body" (1984 61).

Jeremy Bentham's plan for a panoptic prison permits Foucault to discuss the exercise of power in its more diffuse forms. In *Discipline and Punish* he quotes Bentham on the architectural principle on which the panopticon is laid out: At the periphery there is a building shaped like a ring; at the centre there is a *tower* which is pierced with wide windows that open onto the inner side of the ring. The surrounding building is divided into cells, each cell extending the whole width of the building. Cells have two windows, one on the inside, corresponding to the windows of the tower, the other facing outside allowing light to cross the cell from one end to the other (200).

All that is needed to control the inmates (convicts, patients, "madmen," schoolchildren, workers, whoever needs to be put under control) is to place a guard, a supervisor in the central tower. By the effect of full lighting, since one can see way better in full lighting than in darkness, the supervisor in the tower is able to see the inmates in their cells. Each inmate is "caged" alone "perfectly individualized and constantly visible" however this "visibility is a trap" (200). Each inmate isolated in his cell is seen from the front by the supervisor, but the side walls prevent him from coming into contact with other inmates: "He is seen, but he does not see; he is the object of information, never a subject in communication. The arrangement of his room, opposite the central tower, imposes on him an axial visibility; but the divisions of the ring, those separated cells, imply a lateral invisibility" (200). The architectural layout of the prison guarantees order in the inmates' invisibility. Since there is no contact of any kind, and the crowd is replaced by a collection of separated individuals there is no threat to order: "From the point of the guardian, it is replaced by a multiplicity that can be numbered and supervised; from the point of view of the inmates, by a sequestered and observed solitude" (201).

In Bentham's panoptic prison, the inmates have to act as if the guardian is always there watching them. The principles of power as laid out by Bentham are "visibility" and "unverifiability": It should be visible because "the inmate will constantly have before his eyes the tall outline of the central tower from which he is spied upon" (201). It should be unverifiable because "the inmate must never know whether he is being looked at at any one moment; but he must be sure that he may always be so" (201). The inmates' lack of knowledge as to whether the guard is there or not provides the key to the efficiency of the panopticon, since inmates enforce discipline on themselves internalizing the power relations. They take power for granted, comply with it on the seer and seen dichotomy: "The Panopticon is a machine for dissociating the see/being seen dyad: in the peripheric ring, one is totally seen, without ever seeing; in the central tower, one sees everything without ever being seen" (201-202).

In so far as the panopticon "automizes and disindividualizes" power it provides a model that covers the characteristics of a society founded on discipline, *the disciplinary society*. The panopticon "is in fact a figure of political technology" which is a "cruel, ingenious cage" (1975 205). It embodies a system in which surveillance plays an important role, and in which knowledge is inseparably bound to power. To Foucault, the architectural structure of the panopticon serves various techniques of control which would assure the subjection of the inmates almost automatically. He writes that the major effect of the panopticon -where the effects of surveillance is permanent, even if it is not so in its action- is "to induce in the inmate a state of conscious and permanent visibility that assures the automatic functioning of power" (1975 201). Moreover, the panoptic schema is not limited to prisons but it can be applied "whenever one is dealing with a multiplicity of individuals on whom a task or a particular form of behaviour must be imposed" (1975 205).

Foucault talks about the panopticon in later interviews, "Space, Knowledge and Power" (1984), and "The Eye of Power" (1980). In "Space, Knowledge and Power" he contends that architectural form in itself cannot address questions of liberation or oppression, although it could produce "positive effects" when the "liberating intentions of the architect" overlap with "the real practice of people in the exercise of their freedom" (246). This is not a shift in Foucault's thinking since it is not the form of the panopticon which controls the behaviors of inmates, but the power differential between guards and inmates. The form of the building is supporting the exercise of power, hence architecture's capacity to influence human behavior. Moreover, in "The Eye of Power" Foucault holds *spaces* and *powers* as equivalents:

A whole history remains to be written of *spaces*—which would at the same time be the history of *powers* (both these terms in the plural)— from the great strategies of geo-politics to the little tactics of the habitat, institutional architecture from the classroom to the design of hospitals, passing via economic and political installations (149).

Architecture becomes a mode of political organization, which shows that "anchorage in space is an economico-political form" (149):

> [A]rchitecture begins at the end of the eighteenth century to become involved in problems of population, health and the urban question. Previously, the art of building corresponded to the need to make power, divinity and might manifest. The palace and the church were the great architectural forms, along with the stronghold. Architecture manifested might, the Sovereign, God. Its development was for long centred on these requirements. Then, late in the eighteenth century, new problems emerge: it becomes a question of using the disposition of space for economico-political ends (1980 148).

Anchorage in skyscrapers then may prove to be a useful base as a certain type of architectural construction. Although the exterior of a skyscraper is generally the criterion by which its commercial and symbolic success is measured, the interior also proves to be a medium of power and rank, hence "economico-political ends." For example, within the spatial hierarchy of the skyscraper high ranking executive officials claim corner offices, or at least an exterior windowed room, while secretaries and other lower ranking officials are relegated to the deeper, darker spaces (Willis 27). Earle Shultz and Walter Simmons describe the spatially symbolic hierarchy in *Offices in the Sky* (1959):

> Of course the boss had to have his private office next to the window with the light coming in over his shoulder. In some cases his secretary worked in the office, too, but usually she and other clerical help used the reception room space between the private office and the corridor wall. To get maximum light into the reception room, the partition di-

viding it from the private office was glass. Sometimes this glass was opaqued to prevent people waiting in the reception room from seeing into the private office (130).

Even though the main economic reason behind the building of skyscrapers was providing large portions of office space, offices -the interior- were largely ignored because of their powerful exteriors that masked the anonymity of piled up offices. Even a classic movie that came to be instantly associated with the skyscraper like *King Kong* has almost no scene in the interior, save a few seconds shooting the rise of the elevator to the observation deck in Peter Jackson's 2005 remake. The introduction of huge open floor areas for "common" workers, having a sea of desks forms the basis for the hierarchy in the skyscraper form. These open areas have no direct contact with natural light, sporting no windows, no bird's eye view of the city. Everyone working in these almost anonymous areas with co-workers packed, where one's personal space was relegated by either her/his desk or the low rise cubicle panels, desires a more privileged, personal office in the outermost ring. Personal offices of high ranking executives are the opposites of these areas: private offices are separated from the mass of workers either by actual walls or glass panels, they have sunlight and a view, and they are not for "common people." The layout of the open space and its symbolic distance from the private offices are linked in the way that the distinction is a matter of prestige and a matter of control.

As Foucault argues that the panoptic layout is not limited to prisons but it can be applied "whenever one is dealing with a multiplicity of individuals on whom a task or a particular form of behaviour must be imposed" (1975 205), the open space office with its multiplicity of workers who must be docile enough to keep the corporate system going may prove to be an example of spatial dispersal of power relations. As the inmates' lack of knowledge as to whether the guard is in the central tower or not provides the key to the efficiency of Bentham's panopticon, these open spaces offer another diffuse form of coercion in their very openness. The workers like the inmates enforce discipline on themselves internalizing the power relations made possible by the spatial organization of their working place that is essentially separated from executive offices. This time with a reversal, it is not the guard in the central tower, but the executive in the peripheral ring and the peers in the central open area assume the role of the parties in the power play. The seer and seen dyad transforms into another set with the separation of the workers and executives: neither of the parties have direct visual contact by way of their economic and symbolic separation. In the peripheral ring, the executive has total contact with the outside world; in the central area, workers are totally surrounded by walls, caged among a cluster of desks sacrificing any privacy. Insofar as the panopticon disindividualizes power and provides a model for the disciplinary society for Foucault, in the open space office the workers only hope for a leap to the other side of the wall. The architectural structure of the open space serves various techniques of control which would assure the subjection of the workers almost automatically. The major effect of the open space office among peers, where everybody can see and hear anybody, even if it is not so in reality, is a sense of permanent control assuring the internalization of power.

In Mike Nichols's *Working Girl* (1988) for example, Tess McGill (Melanie Griffith) not satisfied with her position as a secretary in the open space, has ambitions to become an executive, having her private office on the perimeter of the skyscraper. Director Nichols sets the movie in a modern skyscraper to reveal the power relations as mediated by built space. Tess looks up to her boss Katherine Parker (Sigourney Weaver) as she goes in and out of her private office. Katherine's office is just a few seconds away from Tess's desk, but the same distance initially seems unbridgeable to Tess, given the cultural capital needed to become an executive. However, by pure coincidence Tess happens to claim Katherine's office: Katherine is involved in an accident and is bedridden for a few weeks and cannot go to work. One day an executive from another firm pays a surprise visit to the office and Tess assumes Katherine's role without any authorization. Tess does a good job in her deception, and by film's end she becomes an executive trainee at another company. When she arrives at her new working place, she sees the same spatial organization, but this time having proved her worth deserves the outer ring offices. Finally the audience sees Tess from her office window, the locus of her newly won victory (Sanders 137).

Clearly spatial organization is a mediator of power relations between executives and their subordinates as is effectively put on screen by Nichols. Only through legitimizing, internalizing the norm can Tess claim a private office for herself. The power of the spatial organization is taken for granted, as Shultz and Simmons say "*Of course* the boss had to have his private office next to the window" (130) [emphasis mine]. In order to have privacy, to have more economic and social power Tess needs to climb the ladder without ever questioning the ways in which herself and her former co-workers have been subjected to spatial coercion. The symbolism of the outer ring office seduces Tess to cross the legitimate line, assuming Katherine's role as an executive. She plays by the rules, and is rewarded with an office of her own in the end. Although her move (like the Foucaultian analysis of power in its disciplinary forms) is notably horizontal in her move from the inside to the periphery, Tess goes *up* in her career, within a symbolic rise in the skyscraper's upward thrust.

As Tess is on her way up, Waring Hudsucker (Charles Durning), the chairman of Hudsucker Industries, literally goes down from a New York skyscraper in Joel and Ethan Coen's *The Hudsucker Proxy* (1994). In the middle of downtown skyscrapers the headquarters of Hudsucker Industries is seen as another "proud and soaring" tower as the camera directs the spectators' gaze from the top of the skyscraper to the bottom. At the bottom stands Norville Barnes (Tim Robbins), another ambitious person ready to go *up* the tower for his first day in Hudsucker Industries. At the top stands the owner of the company and the building, Waring Hudsucker, who is about to jump to his death from the boardroom of the company where all decisions are taken. As the powerful chairman falls, the newcomer begins his ascension to replace him. However, this is not much of an earned success, but a plot devised by the board members led by Sidney Mussburger (Paul Newman) to manipulate stock values and buy the company for a much cheaper price. On his way up, Norville's working space changes accordingly: from the dark, chaotic mailroom to the spacious executive offices (Sanders 121).

These outer ring executive offices with all their imposing power and size are shown to be too distanced from the world below through the simultaneous appearance of Mussburger's silhouette and surrounding skyscrapers' reflections in the top floor boardroom windows. United with the empty, shining surface of the boardroom table, the scene depicts a space of extreme detachment. When Norville designs a circular "thing"- what turns out to be the hula hoop- that the board members agree to manufacture although it seems ridiculous to them, the audience is taken on a tour of the Hudsucker skyscraper: the design department, advertising department, the accounting department, etc. However in the end Mussburger's evil plan works well, and the climax comes with Norville finding himself in the shoes of Waring Hudsucker, the man who was falling when he was about to ascend the tower. For all its layers of irony, the movie takes the audience on a complete tour of the New York skyscraper, inside and out, revealing along the way the profound disunity between the reality of its interior, whose piled up hierarchy of office floors might take a lifetime to climb, and the seductive promise of its exterior that the entire length of the building might be negotiated in a single, breathtaking leap (Sanders 121-123). The symbolic world within the offices of the skyscraper united with its glamorous but deadly façade, reveals a "real" coercive play of power relations for the spectator. Through the gaze of the spectator, the skyscraper proves to be a more than appropriate form of architectural product that directs all attention to the spatial organization as a mediator of power.

Returning to Bentham's panopticon Foucault underlines the significance of *gaze* in the dispersal of the play of powers in their economic and political ends. For him, although posing the problem of visibility, Bentham thinks of a visibility organized entirely around a dominating, overseeing gaze which is an exercise of an "all-seeing power." This is a mode of operation through which power will be exercised through the things being known and people seen in an immediate, collective and anonymous gaze. Surveillance is achieved through the normalizing gaze, which in turn makes the subjects internalize power. Foucault contends that in the system of surveillance

> There is no need for arms, physical violence, material constraints. Just a gaze. An inspecting gaze, a gaze which each individual under its weight will end by interiorising to the point that he is his own overseer, each individual thus exercising this surveillance over, and against, him-

self. A superb formula: power exercised continuously and for what turns out to be a minimal cost. [...] Indeed it is the case that the gaze has had great importance among the techniques of power developed in the modern era (1980 155).

The fiction of a never ending, permanent gaze from the central tower is what makes the subjects docile to the workings of the system at large. A similar process of dispersal of power relations through the impersonal gaze emanates from the distinctive, "central" corporate towers, with a significant difference: here in the vertical urban fabric of the city there is no relying on a single power (the central tower) but a multiplicity of central towers. Spatial domination through grand size or dominant location is able to dwarf the human subject securing compliance to the rules of the game as it points to the power necessary for its production. This is not an overt kind of power one can observe in spatial constructs such as fortresses, but a hidden and silent one operating through the compliance of the subject to surveillance. Spatial domination also seduces, or manipulates the desires of the subject ranging from self-annihilation (as in Stan's suicide in *Manhattan Transfer*) to self-preservation (as in Jimmy's fugue from "the city of destruction") depending on the subject's notion of self identity. This underlines the fact that spatial constructs shape the subject's perception of both her/himself and others. Because distinctive skyscrapers inherently carry the economic power, and the resultant political authority of the corporation or corporations for which they are logos and symbols, the subject feels the urge to share in that power affirming and legitimizing the very authority s/he is put under as s/he participates in its dominance. Each distinctive, landmark skyscraper becomes a mediator of a disciplinary process with its corporate imagery and symbolism of big money intimidating and threatening to cast out those who cannot fight well enough to win for themselves an office space in the higher ground, or a *high* ranking position anywhere as failures. Therefore without ever having to resort to physical violence, a "symbolic violence" in Bourdieu's terms is made manifest.

3.2. Bourdieu and Symbolic Violence

The most successful ideological effects are those that have no words, and ask no more than complicitous silence.

Pierre Bourdieu, Outline of a Theory of Practice, 1977

A work of art has meaning and interest only for someone who possesses the cultural competence, that is, the code [...] The "eye" is a product of history reproduced by education.

Pierre Bourdieu, Distinction, 1979

The symbolic orderings of space and time give profounder continuity to social practices. "Symbolic orderings of space and time provide a framework for experience through which we learn who or what we are in society" writes David Harvey in *The Condition of Postmodernity* adding "the common-sense notion that 'there is a time and a place for everything' gets carried into a set of prescriptions which replicate the social order by assigning social meanings to spaces and times" (214). Bourdieu agrees: "The reason why submission to the collective rhythms is so rigorously demanded is that the temporal forms or the spatial structures structure not only the group's representation of the world but the group itself, which orders itself in accordance with this representation" (1972 163).

Submission to rules is a key point for Bourdieu: "I can say that all of my thinking started from this point: how can behaviour be regulated without being the product of obedience to rules" (1990 65). This is a central theme in Bourdieu's work that questions how human action is regulated and how it is structured without being the product of obedience to norms or conscious intention. In this research the *habitus* becomes a key concept for him.

With *habitus*, Bourdieu refers to the complex net of acquired predispositions into which people are socialized at an early age. For him on the individual level the *habitus* is a "system of acquired dispositions functioning on the practical level as categories of perception and assessment as well as being the organizing principles of action" (1986). In other words, the *habitus* names the cultural categories through which individuals process the world and make decisions about what to do. The *habitus*, then, is a set of practical classifications, divisions and hierarchies which are embedded in everyday life practices. These divisions of space and time, of objects and actions, of gender and status are at once forms of "habit" and "habitat." Therefore, Bourdieu argues in *The Outline of a Theory of Practice* that the *habitus* is embedded in familiar forms such as dwelling and the house is a very important ideological product as the first *habitus*. The *habitus* is:

> a system of lasting, transposable dispositions which integrating past experiences, functions at every moment as a matrix of perceptions, appreciations, and actions and make possible the achievement of infinitely diversified tasks, thanks to analogical transfers of schemes permitting the solution of similarly shaped solutions (Bourdieu, 1971 167).

Thus the *habitus* is a kind of knowledge or belief about the realities of everyday life, although it is a web of acquired dispositions buried deep. It is also a necessary element in any world view; significantly Bourdieu argues in *The Logic of Practice* (1992): "A vision of the world is a division of the world" (210).

The *habitus* is the way the "arbitrary" is constituted as the "real," culture seen as nature, ideology masked in habit and habitat. It constructs one's sense of place in the social and physical senses, as Bourdieu writes in *In Other Words: Essays toward a Reflexive Sociology* (1986): "The habitus produces practices and representations which are available for classification. [...] Thus the habitus implies a 'sense of one's place' but also 'a sense of the other's place.' For example, we say of an item of clothing, a piece of furniture or a book: 'that's petty-bourgeois' or 'that's intellectual'" (113). The power of *habitus* is generated mainly through the fact that it is unconscious. The dominant modes of thought and experience are internalized and embodied. The ideological effects of built form lie largely in this unconscious complex, as Bourdieu writes in *Outline of a Theory of Practice*:

The most successful ideological effects are those that have no words, and ask no more than complicitous silence. It follows, incidentally that any analysis of ideologies, in the narrow sense of "legitimating discourses", which fails to include an analysis of the corresponding institutional mechanisms is liable to be no more than a contribution to the efficacy of those ideologies: this is true of all internal (semiological) analyses of political, educational, religious, or aesthetic ideologies which forget that the political function of these ideologies may in some cases be reduced to the effect of displacement and diversion, camouflage and legitimation, which they produce by reproducing – through their over-sights and omissions, and in their deliberately or involuntarily complicitous silences – the effects of the objective mechanisms (188-189).

Through these "complicitous silences" symbolic violence is made manifest. In *Reproduction In Education, Society and Culture* (1977) Bourdieu and co-author Jean-Claude Passeron define the principal theoretical preposition from which the idea of symbolic violence begins, as such: "Every power to exert symbolic violence, i.e. every power which manages to impose meanings and to impose them as legitimate by concealing the power relations which are the basis of its force, adds its own specifically symbolic force to those power relations" (4). Thus silence and masking; violence passing itself off as legitimate are definitive of symbolic violence. The preposition states the arbitrariness of power relations in that it argues simultaneously the relative autonomy and the relative dependence of symbolic relations with respect to power relations. The authors write in their foreword to the book:

> The term "symbolic violence," which explicitly states the break made with all spontaneous representations and spontaneist conceptions of pedagogic action, recommended itself to us as a means of indicating the theoretical unity of all actions characterized by the twofold arbitrariness of symbolic imposition; it also signifies the fact that this general theory of actions of symbolic violence (whether exerted by the healer, the sorcerer, the priest, the prophet, the propagandist, the teacher, the psychiatrist or the psychoanalyst) belongs to a general theory of violence and legitimate violence, as is directly attested by the in-

terchangeability of the different forms of social violence and indirectly by the homology of legitimate symbolic violence and the state's monopoly of the legitimate use of physical violence (1977 xi-xii).

Bourdieu's sociology of education is like an extension of his theory of practice with the *habitus*, to form a general theory of symbolic violence. The authors specify the processes in which order and social restraint are produced by indirect, cultural mechanisms rather than by direct coercive social control. According to Bourdieu, symbolic violence "is the imposition of systems of symbolism and meaning (i.e. culture) upon groups or classes in such a way that they are experienced as legitimate" (Jenkins 104). It is this legitimacy that obscures power relations which allow that imposition to be successful. As long as it is perceived as legitimate, culture adds its own force to those power relations, contributing to their systematic *reproduction*. Cultural reproduction contributes to maintaining the power of dominant groups. Significantly this is achieved through *misrecognition* (mèconnaissance): "the process whereby power relations are perceived not for what they objectively are but in a form which renders them legitimate in the eyes of the beholder" (Bourdieu and Passeron xiii).

The central cohesive source of support for the exercise of symbolic violence is "pedagogic action." Pedagogic action reproduces culture, and also reproduces the power relations which underline its own operation. Pedagogic actions reflect the interests of dominant groups or classes, tending to reproduce the uneven distribution of cultural capital among these groups or classes which inhabit the social space in question, hence reproducing social structure (Jenkins 105).

Bourdieu's concept of symbolic violence is something intangible as opposed to physical violence. It is more powerful than physical violence in that it is invisible and unintelligible. "Ol mahiler ki derya içredir deryayı bilmezler" [the fish in the sea does not know about the sea] says sixteenth century Ottoman poet Hayali Bey, implying the insensitivity of the subject to stimulants around himself through prolonged exposure. This disinterestedness of the subject translates itself as a *blasé* attitude in the city, as Georg Simmel had it in his

"The Metropolis and Mental Life" (1903). Simmel defines the essence of blasé attitude as "an indifference toward the distinctions between things. Not in the sense that they are not perceived, as is the case of mental dullness, but rather that the meaning and the value of distinctions between things, and therewith of the things themselves, are experienced as meaningless" (35-36).

Like the fish in the sea who does not know about the sea, big city dwellers have been living through all kinds of inhibition and suppression without ever knowing, or acknowledging them, preferring most of the time to adopt a cold, blasé attitude. It is this quality of symbolic violence that gives it its unique power. Individuals are often victims of this symbolic power, but they are not able to realize it, or more than that they are not aware of the fact that they are subjected to symbolic violence because they do not know any other way other then submission to the perceived general hegemony of the norm. Dangerous as it is most of the time in not recognizing the symbolic violence, however it is more often the case that people prefer not to act against it often because they do not possess the "cultural capital" needed to do so. It is also probable that they had internalized it to such a high degree that they desire to be a part of the system of symbolic power, striving to become one of the aggressors in climbing up the social/economic ladder and doing what it takes to realize the American Dream of material success. It is important to underline that this is specifically an "alladoxia"[7] in Bourdieu's terms.

It is through the largeness and tallness, the symbolic power of the skyscrapers that people come to be exposed to symbolic violence in the American context, most effective in New York City's Manhattan. As was previously stated skyscrapers were responses to market pressure for more rentable space on a given site area; however there are physical limits to this increase in site efficiency:

> As a long thin building serviced entirely from one tip, the tower as a type also loses efficiency with height. The necessary service core expands exponentially in relation to the floor area since every additional floor requires an increment of service core to every floor beneath.

---
[7] Bourdieu's term for misrecognition.

Banks of elevators progressively consume the building volume until every new floor at the top consumes more service core than it adds in usable space. When this effect is coupled with parking requirements at the base, the tower reaches a point where the cost of increased height exceeds the gains in rental area (Dovey 107).

Given the functional inefficiencies, it would be logical for one to expect that the race for the tallest skyscraper would slow down, but it does not. The proliferation of corporate skyscrapers then would depend not on a functional reason but a symbolic one: that of "symbolic capital" in Bourdieu's terms.

Capital is an economic concept that refers to the machines, plants and buildings used in the industrial manufacturing process, and technically it is one of the four factors of production, others being land, labor, and entrepreneurship. A factor of production is a resource that is valued for its function in the production of goods and services. Capital is any resource or item used in the production process that has already been subject to some form of productive labor. From a Marxist view, capitalism, where capital plays a predominant role in the economic production process, is theorized in terms of the organization of production and the resultant relationship between economic classes, namely the bourgeoisie which owns and controls the means of production and the proletariat that owns only its ability to work, surviving by selling its labor power. However, Bourdieu extends the idea of capital to all forms of power, not just to economic power as does Marxist theory. Bourdieu sees power as diffuse or symbolic which is often masked in generally accepted and often taken for granted ways of seeing and defining the world like Foucault does. Bourdieu regards this symbolic power intertwined with economic and political power thereby serving a legitimating function. Foucault also sees the state as extremely important, although his work represents a challenge to conventional political theory. In *Discipline and Punish* he seems vague about economics and comes close, in his ambivalence, to saying that power is concerned with the maximization of productive forces. Although Foucault never dismisses the economic element of power, he also does not privilege it as the basis of power.

Individuals and groups draw upon a variety of cultural, social, and symbolic resources in order to maintain and enhance their positions in the social order. Bourdieu conceptualizes such resources as capital when they function as a "social relation of power," that is when they become objects of struggle as valued resources. In modern societies access to sources of income in the labor market depends on "cultural capital" in the form of educational credentials, and "social capital" in the form of networks (Swartz 73-74). In "Forms of Capital" (1986) Bourdieu argues that there are four generic types of capital: economic capital (money and property), cultural capital (cultural goods and services, education as an investment), social capital (acquaintances and networks), and symbolic capital (legitimation) (243).

Roughly symbolic capital is the value that can be attributed to a symbolic, aesthetic or mythological "aura." It is a form of power that is exercised through "an action of knowledge" which "enables one to account for the relations of force that are actualized in and by relations of cognition (or recognition) and of communication" (Bourdieu, 1999 336). For Bourdieu, the logic of the symbolic is fundamentally diacritical (distinguishing), and distinction is the specific form of profit that symbolic capital procures:

> Lifestyle, as the exemplary manifestation of symbolic capital, exists only by and for the *gaze* of the other and as diacritical deviation from the modal, ordinary, common, banal, "average" style, a deviation that can be unwitting or obtained by a "stylization of life." The symbolic profit of distinction (which can be reconverted into material profits) results, apart from any intentional pursuit, from the monopolistic possession (exclusivity) of some species of capital and from the *exhibition*, intentional or not, of this capital and of the difference attached to its possession (Bourdieu, 1999 337) [emphases mine].

Thus, symbolic capital significantly works within the field of vision; it needs to be exhibited to such a great degree so as to be seen by others. It is in the exhibitionism of the skyscraper with its largeness and tallness that cannot escape the gaze of observers, lies its symbolic power. "The successful corporate tower offers corporate identity, authenticity and authority. It embodies metaphors of strength, stature and strategy, of physical dominance translating into financial domination" (Dovey 4). The aura that the skyscraper generates is its symbolic capital. Although growing tallness is not an element that increases the skyscraper's efficiency, each and every day a new project for "the tallest building in the world" makes its way to the headlines. It is the image, the symbolic capital of a skyscraper that will distinguish it from other skyscrapers and give it a market advantage for rental: The successful corporate tower offers a distinctive image to which lessees are invited to link their corporate image. Distinction is also achieved through a quest for uniqueness of form whether viewed in the city skyline or in relation to neighboring buildings. The ideal tower is a landmark in the literal sense of leaving a mark on the land (Dovey 108-109). If a building leaves a mark on the land it becomes monumental. If it becomes monumental, it has more ability to exert more "symbolic violence." It is the case with all distinctive skyscrapers of New York like the early Singer, Met Life, and Woolworth Buildings; the Chrysler and Empire State of the 1930s; and World Trade Center of 1970s, which were the world's tallest buildings successively. However, it is only through the "twin towers" of the World Trade Center that symbolic violence turns into physical violence as exemplified in their destruction claiming nearly three thousand lives as a consequence of terrorist attacks in September 11, 2001.

4. SEPTEMBER 11 AND FALL OF THE TWIN TOWERS

> *To fill a Gap*
> *Insert the Thing that caused it—*
> *Block it up*
> *With Other –and 'twil yawn the more—*
> *You cannot solder an Abyss*
> *With Air.*
>
> Emily Dickinson

Freudian and Lacanian psychoanalytic theory describes desire as an orientation toward something the subject is lacking and implies the existence of an active drive: looking for something to fill that lack. However, this "something" the subject is looking for can never be attained. Although the absent father is substituted by a leader, a common ideal or an object the idea of an originary father still underlines the loss. Freud argues that the libido is the subjective essence of desire, and in the Oedipal stage sexual impulses drive the child to fulfill a role within the familial structure through the establishment of sexual relationships that give way to conflicts within the subject. Freud uses the constitution of desire within the Oedipal triangle to theorize desire as lack that the subject attempts to fill. Formulated under the constant threat of castration, desire becomes a self-destructive force that also constitutes life.

Further, as Lacan argues in a Hegelian dialectic of the master and slave; the desire of the subject is always the desire of the Other, of the Other's desire for recognition. Lacan argues in "The Subversion of the Subject and the Dialectic of Desire in the Freudian Unconscious" (1960) that "desire becomes bound up at that junction with the Other's desire" (289). Since desire is necessarily a lack, the absent, "dead Father" of Freud who could be regarded as the original representative of the Law's authority ("no" or "nom" of the father: Name-of-the-Father) sustains himself beyond the subject who is led to really occupy the place of the Other, namely, the Mother (Lacan, 1960 298-299). Mother's lack of a penis, her desire to have/to be the phallus is the condition that directs the child to look for this missing –though imaginary- phallus, trying to become the phallus: "it is the absence of the penis that makes her the phallus, the object of desire" (Lacan, 1960 310). Hence, "the Other's desire that man's desire takes shape" (Lacan, 1960 299). This way desire presents itself as free of the Law's mediation, because Law is engendered by desire and the true function of the Father is not to oppose a desire to the Law, but to unite the desire to the Law. Insofar as "there is no Other of the Other" (Lacan, 1960 303) lack becomes central in the formation of the subject which is regulated by the threat of castration; it is castration that regulates desire (Lacan, 1960 311).

In Freudian and Lacanian psychoanalysis, it is the constant threat of rupture, of castration that the phallus takes on its symbolic function, and the phallus is thus always a reactive and defensive construct: if it claims the status of a transhistorical truth, this is always in some fraught relationship to the sense in which it is imagined to be "under attack." Therefore, the phallus is not a timeless entity with no historical content but a kind of hastily improvised patchwork of historical materials that might vary according to historical contingencies: the mournful reassertion of national identity in the wake of World War I, the reassertion of a triumphant global capitalist order in the face of attacks on it in September 11, 2001.

If it is a patchwork, it would become impossible to assert that the phallus represents any one thing monolithically. To call it a phallus seems necessarily to imply that it has a gendered meaning, but this would have to be seen as overdetermined by other elements such as national identity, capitalism and the like in ways which would make any reading of it necessarily a tracing of those polysemantic overdeterminations. In tracing the functional, historic, psychological and symbolic ends that the phallic skyscraper form serves, the study at hand lays out these polysemantic overdeterminations. Insofar as the skyscrapers of Manhattan exhibit and engender desire and power through the dominant phallic and therefore a visual spatiality, the dispersal of power in its diffuse and symbolic forms are manifested through the idea of the phallus.

The threat of castration or rupture is in fact the lack of center and origin that makes any structure a site of eternal deferral of meaning. Rupture thus drives the productive nature of structure and makes meaning possible as a dynamic process at the same time as it makes meaning indeterminate. Just as for Freud the phallus might be seen as always reflecting and repeating the very loss of the father that it tries to cover over, rupture re-emerges at every moment through the deferral of meaning rather than being some moment of originary or archetypal loss. What one might object to Freud is the fact that the connection of the phallus as the arbitrator of meaning to the determinate element of the penis is in itself the "erection" of a center and "prototype" of loss, for which all other losses then only become figures or copies. There can be no original loss which predetermines the nature of those that follow. But this is compatible with the historicist reading of towers.

A historicist reading of towers represents a kind of phallocentric and phonocentric assertion of center and presence over dispersal (that of different languages, for example), but they would in fact never be able to effect a recapture of a mythic lost plenitude of self-presence of meaning. Each is "only a copy." But this does not mean that each tower conjures up a long "tradition" of previous towers thus makes on a more flexible and fraught meaning: each attempts to master the very tradition that makes it belated rather than, in itself the origin of the tradition. The tradition would be conjured up with each repetition, but it would be a kind of defensive reassertion of a tradition with no origins and no foundations. The repetition would displace the very myth of origins. The re-assertion of a mythic center and a nostalgia for a point of origin which is in fact empty so that each repetition can only repeat the origin in a movement of displacing and decentering.

4.1. The Twin Towers

Skyscrapers go up like flames, in flames, flames.

John Dos Passos, *Manhattan Transfer*, 1925

In the uncanny doubleness of the Twin Towers whose fall came to be the very symbols of the attacks in September 11, no originary reference remains. Baudrillard writes prophetically in 1983 in his *Simulations*:

The fact that there are two of them signifies the end of all competition, the end of all original reference. [...] What they project is the idea of the model that they are one for the other, and their twin altitude presents no longer any value of transcendence. They signify only that the strategy of models and commutations wins out in the very heart of the system itself –and New York is really the heart of it- over the traditional strategy of competition (135-136).

Indeed when the project of a World Trade Center was being worked out during the 1960s, it was intended to put an end to all competition. The proposal for the World Trade Center reads: "Today, the world stands on the brink of a boom in international trade. [...] To realize its role in the new era dawning for overseas trade and finance, this country must marshal its resources. One primary step in this direction would be to establish *a single center*, planned and equipped to serve that vital purpose" (quoted in Glanz and Lipton 7) [emphasis mine]. The idea of a "single center" does not only refer to the proposed buildings themselves but also to the country and the city they were going to be built in.

The World Trade Center has been the symbol of U.S. economic strength. In the 60s Chase Manhattan Bank's Chairman David Rockefeller and his brother governor of New York State Nelson Rockefeller initiated the foundation of Port Authority of New York and New Jersey to commission a development project that would revitalize downtown New York which had been the financial center of the country. In 1962 architect Minoru Yamasaki was hired to head the design. Although Yamasaki believed that "If a building is too strong or brutal, it tends to overpower man. In it he feels insecure and uncomfortable" (quoted in Glanz and Lipton 88) he designed two identical, huge, excessively simple glass boxes. A great majority of the public and architectural critics protested these huge monoliths that cut off human activity on the streets, but they were also driven to it by its very height and identical doubleness. Therefore, not curiously enough, Michel de Certeau begins his chapter "Walking in the City" in *The Practice of Everyday Life* (1984) as such:

Seeing Manhattan from the 110th floor of the World Trade Center. Beneath the haze stirred up by the winds, the urban island, a sea in the middle of the sea, lifts up the skyscrapers over Wall Street, sinks down at Greenwich, then rises again to the crests of Midtown, quietly passes over Central Park and finally undulates off into momentarily arrested vision. The gigantic mass is immobilized before the eyes" (91).

Thus the city turns into a text with the view from the tallest tower of the city. Being lifted up, means being "lifted out of the city's grasp" (92) out of its streets. With the panoptic, all-seeing, god-like eye that encompasses the whole city the subject on top of the tower assumes the power of the structure. The cityscape from the tower transforms the walking subject, the pedestrian, into a *voyeur*. It is clear that de Certeau draws on psychoanalysis and Foucault in his reworking of the interrelationship between power relations, the built environment, the subject and the visual field. De Certeau invokes the scopic drive or "scopophilia" as Freud formulated it in "Three Essays on the Theory of Sexuality" (1905).

It is in the skyscraper's exhibition of corporate power and wealth that they draw the subject's desire to look. In the essays Freud argues that "visual impressions remain the most frequent pathway along which libidinal excitation is aroused" (Freud 69). Pleasure in looking becomes a perversion, according to Freud, in the form of voyeurism and its double exhibitionism: "anyone who is an exhibitionist in his unconscious is at the same time a *voyeur*" (81). Freud's formulation as reworked by Lacan in the split between the organic eye and the gaze takes on a significant plane in respect to towers. The towers with their soaring height incorporate a panoptic view of the city, gazing back at the walking subject. The gaze on part of the tower is aggressive since it belittles the one on the street, hence pouring out symbolic violence. This process is further underlined by Freud's assertion that the force which opposes "scopophilia" is shame (Freud, 1905 69). The towers of Manhattan are also voyeurs gazing back at the subject and exhibitionists in their "unashamed" display of power. This becomes more forceful in the case of the World Trade Center as the peak of the vertical city, and as "the most monumental figure of Western urban development" (de Certeau 93).

Underlining the monumental aspect the Twin Towers reached a hundred and ten stories replacing the Empire State Building as the tallest, although supertall skyscrapers do not make much economic sense as was discussed before. Indeed, after their completion in 1972 and 1973 the Twin Towers became the world's tallest buildings, only to be replaced by Chicago's Sears Tower a year later. Although they were no longer the world's tallest, they were the world's largest in terms of rentable office space until their destruction. They stood taller than any other skyscraper in New York's skyline and conveyed a symbolic message of American success and achievement. They stood as a symbol of America's financial power and as a symbol of American culture. *Washington Post* columnist Benjamin Forgey suggests that, "buildings –their shapes, materials, textures and spaces– represent culture in its most persuasive physical form. Destroy the buildings, and you rob a culture of its memory, of its legitimacy, of its right to exist" (www.washingtonpost.com). After their destruction the Twin Towers came to represent destruction and terror in a city traumatized by the unprecedented attacks.

The fall of the Twin Towers has been often referred to as a reminder of the Tower of Babel. It is important to remember why people had built the Tower of Babel: To preserve their name, and to avoid being scattered in judgment. Here one might see the principle behind the first and not the last tower: whenever human beings seek to reassert their own imaginary power and authority (phallus) they again and again construct a tower, a defense against the threat of castration in the form of a fetish object. As Freud explains in "Fetishism" (1927), the fetish is a substitute for the phallus: the woman's (the mother's) penis that the little boy once believed in and does not want to give up. The fetish achieves a token of triumph over the threat of castration and serves as a protection against it, which necessarily implies a split in the subject's ego (952-956). However, the indeterminacy and overdetermination of the idea of the phallus should be underlined. Since the decenteredness of this idea can further thoughts about the precise ways in which Twin Towers functioned as a symbol not transhistorically but rather much more contingently in terms of national fetish, imagined "center" of a decentered and non-territorial global capitalism.

4.2. The Politics of "Mourning and Melancholia" after September 11

The hijacked planes of American Airlines Flight 11 and United Airlines Flight 175 crashed into and destroyed the World Trade Center towers in New York on September 11, 2001 killing about three thousand people. They were not the only hijacked planes that day; American Airlines Flight 77 crashed into the Pentagon in Washington, D.C. and United Airlines Flight 93 crashed in Shanksville, Pennsylvania. However, it was the fall of the Twin Towers of the World Trade Center that came to be a synecdoche for the whole of September 11.

Since the attack on Pearl Harbor during World War II the United States had not experienced a "foreign" attack on its territory. But the attacks of September 11 were different from the attack on Pearl Harbor: First, it was not a time of war; second New York City was not a military base; third Pearl Harbor was part of Hawaii which was not a state in the union yet, rather it was an official U.S. territory like Puerto Rico today; fourth the United States was not a "superpower" back then. Therefore, the effects of the attack on Pearl Harbor on the public felt less immediate than the attacks of September 11.

With the sudden, unexpected loss of both the towers and the lives of people in them, the American public succumbed into a national melancholia. In "Mourning and Melancholia" (1917) Freud defines mourning as "the reaction to the loss of a loved person, or to the loss of some abstraction which has taken the place of one, such as one's country, liberty, an ideal, and so on" (243). However, in some people the same influences produce melancholia instead of mourning which Freud sees as a pathology: The distinguishing mental features of melancholia are a profoundly painful depression, an end of interest in the outside world, loss of the capacity to love, inhibition to all activity, and a lowering of the self-regarding feelings to a degree that finds utterance in self-reproaches and self-reviling, and culminates in a delusional expectation of punishment (244). The features of melancholia are the same with that of mourning except an extraordinary lowering of self-regard: In mourning it is the world which has become poor and empty; in melancholia it is the ego itself" (246). Self-criticism takes over anything else in melancholia making the superego talk lauder and more aggressively on moral grounds. Melancholia borrows some of its features from mourning, and the others from the process of regression from narcissistic object choice to narcissism (250-258).

Then, as opposed to melancholia, successful mourning means the exchange of the lost object with another object. However, Freud changes his mind on the distinction between mourning and melancholia after five years in *The Ego and the Id*, where the two become intermingled. Before he had hold that it was only in melancholia that an object which was lost had been set up again inside the ego, through the subject's "incorporation" of the lost object inside her/his body, but now he holds that rebuilding the lost object is also essential for the process of mourning (23). Fusion of mourning and melancholia also parallels the replacement of object choice by identification, whereby the subject assimilates an aspect of the external object rebuilt in the ego. This readily evokes Freud's discussion of narcissism and object choice in group psychology, where it is the external object which is put in place of the ego ideal of the group.

As the ego ideal of a nation, their being the embodiment of the country's economic and political strength the Twin Towers' loss engenders such a "national melancholia." The argument follows Judith Butler's discussion of the task of mourning after September 11, and the American government's violence that followed it, in *Precarious Life: The Powers of Mourning and Violence* (2004). Butler takes up a psychoanalytic understanding of loss that quickly results in aggression. Following Freud's account of mourning, Butler formulates "national melancholia" as a disavowed mourning that follows upon the absence of those who are killed by the U.S. military intervention after September 11. Butler argues that only U.S.'s own losses are presented as "livable lives" and "grievable deaths" by the media and the government.

Although the perpetrators of the September 11 attacks have never been fully identified with sound proofs (at least to the international community), and no evidence of a single mass destruction weapon has been found in Iraq, a border between patriot and enemy was already drawn immediately after the attacks by the American government. The American government construed the attacks as attacks on "freedom," on "American values," on the "American way of life." According to the official narrative it was the "American culture" that was attacked. Then in the light of the official rhetoric, American culture, as symbolized by the Twin Towers, is one of neo-liberal global capitalism. As nothing seems to be weakening the "anonymous centers" of deterritorialized global capitalism, the fallen Twin Towers are being replaced by even higher towers. Indeed as Žižek writes, the real politico-ideological catastrophe of September 11 was not that of the U.S., on the contrary: "the result of September 11 is an unprecedented strengthening of American hegemony, in all its aspects" (2002 144).

About a week after the attacks, on September 20 U.S. President George W. Bush declared it was time to put an end to mourning and go after revenge: "Our grief has turned to anger, and anger to resolution. Whether we bring our enemies to justice, or bring justice to our enemies, justice will be done" (www.whitehouse. gov). The U.S. government's proposal for a premature recovery from mourning finds its aggressive outlet in a sadistic push to not only cast out or castrate those outside the group, but to annihilate them. Freud defines sadism as the ultimate death instinct "which has been directed outward" towards an external object (1923). Bush redefines this in a dichotomy of "we" against "them": You are either with us or against us; if you are not with us you will have to endure the consequences; we lost lives, so will you. In the final analysis, what Bush offers is an anchorage in a renunciation of mourning. Butler concludes: "When grieving is something to be feared, our fears can give rise to the impulse to resolve it quickly, to banish it in the name of an action invested with the power to restore the loss or return the world to a former order, or to reinvigorate a fantasy that the world formerly was orderly" (29-30). The former world was of a United States that was not breached by the Other. In the loss of what Butler calls the "First Worldism," Americans had to come to terms with the fact that the former order of a country that "transgresses the sovereign boundaries of other states, but never be in the position of having [its] own boundaries transgressed" (Butler 39) was radically changed. What the American public needed was not the abandoning of healthy mourning in favor of violent revenge.

Immature "recovery" from loss also resulted in a radical desire for security as was exemplified by the so-called "PATRIOT Act" proposed by the Republican government and passed with a strong backing from the Democrats. In the early months after September 11, there seemed to be a non-partisan approach to the events. It was considered "un-American" to blame the U.S. government and the rhetoric of the "War on Terror." Those who dared to criticize the actions taken by the government have been stigmatized as enemies clearly seen in the banning of Susan Sontag, Arundhati Roy, Noam Chomsky and other critical intellectuals from the mainstream media. Even the American Studies Department at New York University that included faculty who publicly criticized the government was sent a mail that contained a yellow substance made to look like anthrax. The mail was addressed to the "Un-American Studies Department" at NYU.

In the common enemy a narrative of solidarity and strength arose in popular banners like "United We Stand," although initially the attacks challenged the sense of hubris or complacency that many Americans had come to think and believe that the country as the world superpower was indestructible. After September 11 both public and legislative attitudes towards safety have become central issues, making national and personal security key points as government and media sponsored fears of similar attacks increased. This was especially evident in the rhetoric of the 2004 presidential election for both candidates (Benedetto and Lawrence 2004). Indeed, the general sentiment was that a terrorist attack was not a matter of possibility, but a matter of time as the U.S. President Bush was quoted as saying: "it's not if, but when." This kind of rhetoric comes from a desire to put forward a totalizing response to movements that stimulated the attacks of September 11, and in this sense the dominant cultural narratives of the event produce new forms of violence born from supposedly ethical justifications rationalized by the claim of "self-defense" (Butler 39). The fact is with the PATRIOT Act at home, with Guantanamo and military responses abroad, the U.S. government has enacted an equally ideological violence with that of the terrorists.

Beginning particularly with Marx and Engels's *The German Ideology* (1845), ideology has been considered a perplexing lens that distorts people's perception of an objective reality. The ruling class (those in control of material production) determines the ruling intellectual force of a given social arrangement (Marx and Engels, 64). Ideology never calls itself ideology, rather it is always an accusation directed towards an other (Althusser 164). In explaining how subjects become trapped within webs of domination, Althusser's notion of "interpellation" is helpful. With interpellation, Althusser conceptualizes a transformation that turns individuals to subjects (164). He calls this operation "hailing," which starts identification on the part of the individual who understands a communicative act as being addressed to her/him rather than someone else. Althusser explains this as "along the lines of the most commonplace everyday police (or other) hailing: 'Hey, you there!' [...] the hailed individual will turn round [...] Because he has recognized that the hail was 'really' addressed to him" (164). After September 11, such hailing has emerged in the form of grim pictures of death (people falling from the Twin Towers) and heroism (rescue workers, firefighters and police) alongside one another as sources of union, to the exclusion of the other. A sense of xenophobia began to pervade in the public, amounting to the killing of a Sikh who was mistaken for an Arab because he was wearing a turban. Amidst this racist sentiment a call for multicultural tolerance was issued. However, behind the multicultural tolerance is an "inverted, self-referential form of racism" that affirms the universality of the white western voice (Žižek, 1997 44). Tolerance in its very essence is the power play by those who are deemed to have the capacity to value or devalue different subjectivities.

Further, in legislative moves that aim ultimately at censorship even in the subjective realm, the U.S. government affirms the exclusion of any dissident activity as unpatriotic. Eli Zaretsky argues that the government reaction to attacks on September 11 "disrupted the most fundamental ontological structure on which all security depends: that of the public/private division" (2002 101). The PATRIOT Act, the short form of "Uniting and Strengthening America by **P**roviding **A**ppropriate **T**ools **R**equired to **I**ntercept and **O**bstruct **T**errorism" was passed in the fall of 2001. Within the framework of the act, the basic requirements for identifying and eliminating possible threats dissolve the distinction between the private and the public, so that the private becomes public as Elaine Scrarry explains:

> The objective of the Patriot Act becomes even clearer if it is understood concretely as making the population *visible* and the Justice Department *invisible*. The Act inverts the constitutional requirements that people's lives be private and the work of government officials be public; it instead crafts a set of conditions that make our inner lives transparent and the workings of the government opaque (16).

Scarry adds that the PATRIOT Act violates the First, Fourth, Fifth, Sixth, Eighth, and Fourteenth Amendments alternately and that it defines the patriotic citizen as essentially a compliant and docile body (16). With the PATRIOT Act, the "private" ceases to exist: federal officers may "enter and search a person's house, [...] survey private medical records, business records, library records, and educational records, and [...] monitor telephone, email and Internet use" (Scarry 17).

Moreover, in New York for example, citizens are invited to *watch and report* any suspicious behavior; a potentially dangerous person, object or activity by signs that still appear in the subways: "If you see something, say something" reads the signs which also appear in Spanish: "Ves algo, di algo." Therefore, under the PATRIOT Act, not only submission to the rules but also active participation in the application of the norm is also called for, whereby subjects are expected to agree to become the "I" or the "eye" of the state. This also implies that the "evil other" is a threat that is located within the country; it can be anyone, the person sitting next to you in the train could very well be a terrorist. A culture of paranoia is thus set free.

4.3 Rebuilding the Phallus: The Freedom Tower

The threat of terrorism has enabled the American administration after September 11 to enact surveillance with minimal protest from its subjects. Public and official reaction to architect Daniel Libeskind's winning plan for the rebuilding of Ground Zero, and the architect's own vision as displayed by the plan suggest some of the means by which the terrorist attacks in New York have been internalized and by which the plan reflects an architectural power play between the attackers and the attacked. The study at hand reads architecture and the rebuilding plan for Ground Zero as a political act, because "The World Trade Center was the eye of a needle through which global capital flowed, the seat of an empire. However anonymous they appeared, the Twin Towers were never benign, never just architecture. Recovering this site for the living city is, therefore, inescapably political" (Sorkin and Zukin xi).

In the history of constructing high buildings the latest chain of the line is evident in New York City's redevelopment plans for Ground Zero, the site where the Twin Towers of the World Trade Center once stood "erect." Within two months after the attacks the governor of New York George Pataki established a new state agency responsible for overseeing the rebuilding process: Lower Manhattan Development Corporation (LMDC). LMDC's motto "Remember, Rebuild, Renew" underlines the desire to restore the phallus. LMDC Chairman John Whitehead said as he introduced the preliminary proposals for rebuilding the World Trade Center site: "We will rebuild. It is now not a question of whether, but a question of how" (www.cnnstudentnews. cnn.com/TRANSCRIPTS/0207 /16/wbr.00.html). Moreover, LMDC states its mission as "ensuring Lower Manhattan recovers from the attacks and emerges *even better than it was before* [...] *restoring a powerful, tall symbol in Lower Manhattan's skyline*" (www.renewnyc.org) [emphasis mine]. Thus what Libeskind proposes is this phallic symbol embodied in the new tower, dubbed the "Freedom Tower" by Governor Pataki. This "powerful, tall symbol" will be 1,776-feet-tall, symbolizing the year of American independence. It will be the tallest building in the western hemisphere, that will be about 400 feet taller than the original Twin Towers, and about 100 feet taller than Taipei 101 of Taiwan (1,667 ft), the tallest of the world as of 2006.

As Larry Silverstein, a real estate developer, who had leased the Twin Towers a few weeks before the attacks, began to put on more pressure economic worries have taken hold of the project. Also for security reasons Libeskind's plan was changed by David Childs of Skidmore, Owings & Merril who had been working for Silverstein from the beginning. With the changes, causing intense fights between Childs and Libeskind, the plan no longer has the slurry wall, the gardens, and the spire is replaced by an antenna tower. Libeskind is now only referred to as the master planner, David Childs is responsible for overseeing the rebuilding on behalf of Silverstein. However, as the rebuilding physically began only in the spring of 2006 no one can be sure what other changes might be done to the project. Therefore, though recognizing the fact that the original plan has been altered radically, the study at hand takes the original design as proposed by Libeskind as its basis.

In the "Design Plan for Freedom Tower" Libeskind assures the LMDC that the new tower will become a "lasting icon and a symbol of renewal" to "recapture the skyline and establish a new civic icon for this city and our country" (www.renewnyc.org/plan_des_dev/wtc-site/new_design_plans/freedom_tower_dec_19.asp). "The impulse to rebuild instantly captured the public imagination as an opportunity to express the resolve of the nation. Ground Zero, in other words, is already an ideologically charged site (Ross 127). Indeed in its report "A Vision for Lower Manhattan" (2002), LMDC sets out the very ideology of the rebuilding the tower: The design should serve the goal to underline the status of New York City as the destination of a pagan pilgrimage, as the destination of a quest for material success. Hence LMDC's chosen plan, which "preserves and reveals the slurry walls of the bathtub of the World Trade Center site as a symbol and physical embodiment of the resilience of American democracy and freedom in withstanding the attacks of September 11th 2001" (www.renewnyc.org/Content/AvisionforLower Manhattan.pdf) is another architectural venture to rebuild the lost object of mourning in the form of an ego ideal in New York City.

For the Polish-Jewish-American architect Daniel Libeskind, buildings are not inanimate objects, they live and breathe, and "every building tells a story, or better yet, several stories. [...] A great building, like great literature or poetry or music, can tell the story of the human soul" (Libeskind 3, 4). Libeskind writes in his "architectural autobiography," *Breaking Ground* (2004) that as the son of two Holocaust survivors, because of "who he is" he has thought a lot about trauma and memory (12). Trauma and memory, and the inescapable void guide his design of the Jewish Museum in Berlin, and his master plan for Ground Zero.

His "nomadic life" as he calls it, with his parents' search for a home takes the family from Poland to the Soviet Union, back to Poland, then to Israel only to be at home in New York in 1959 when he was thirteen. Libeskind writes: "We were Israelites, arriving in the Promised Land, but we were also Joseph, leaving it. Our real promised land would be New York City" (2004 32-33). His remembrance of the family's arrival in New York has proved to be an important topic he often recalled in his speeches about the rebuilding plans. "If you are an immigrant kid, it is the most incredible sight: Lady Liberty pointing her torch to the sky. You behold the promise that awaits you. As for the skyline, the tremendous success story of America is almost palpable in its grandeur" (33). He explains his experience and its effects on his architecture:

> As an immigrant, whose youth often felt displaced, I sought to create a different architecture, one that reflects an understanding of history after world catastrophes. I find myself drawn to explore what I call the void—the presence of an overwhelming emptiness created when a community is wiped out, or individual freedom is stamped out; when community life is so brutally disrupted that the structure of life is forever torqued and transformed" (12).

The guiding idea for Libeskind's plan for rebuilding Ground Zero, which he calls "The Memory Foundations," is a new architecture based on "democratic ideals" (43) embodied in his childhood remembrance of the Statue of Liberty. However, for Libeskind, in recapturing a sense of place and history buildings should never be nostalgic; they should speak to the present and the future:

> I am inspired by light, sound, invisible spirits, a distinct sense of place, a respect for history. We are all shaped by a constellation of realities and invisible forces, and if a building is to have a spiritual resonance, it has to reflect these things. No one knows how body and soul are connected, but connect them is what I try to do. I draw from my own experience—it's what I know—and in doing so, I strive for a universality (Libeskind 16).

Therefore what Libeskind sought to propose for Ground Zero was a future having strong footing in history. This is also an economic history, because with the fall of the Twin Towers downtown Manhattan lost ten million square feet of rentable office space. Since Ground Zero is in the heart of Manhattan's financial district "it was psychologically as well as economically vital to provide the area with a future, to move on from its traumatic past" (Libeskind, 2004 38). To move on, recreating the past[8] was wrong, what was called for was a reinterpretation. Libeskind implies that he did not want to make the same mistake Yamasaki did back in the 60s, or competing architects were doing in building a soaring, mega-structure that cut off life in the streets surrounding the building although they were revealing a strong sense of individuality, which is one of the basic tenets of American culture. He writes "[m]y aim was to mold the site into a coherent and symbolic whole by designing buildings that would ascend gradually in pattern. And I wanted not to build just another isolated building there, but to create a new neighborhood, a new harmonious community" (2004 46).

With "Memory Foundations" Libeskind achieves three goals: he reserves the memory, looks into the future integrating life in the street to the building, and recreates the lost office space. By keeping the original slurry wall of the Twin Towers he creates a living memorial, because the slurry wall is "a metaphoric and a literal stay against chaos and destruction. In refusing to fall, it seemed to attest, perhaps as eloquently as the Constitution, to the unshakable foundations of democracy and the value of human life and liberty" (Libeskind, 2004 43). He remembers telling the audience in the Winter Garden of the World Financial Center where the final six proposals for Ground Zero is first made public in 2002:

> I told them about what Nina [his wife] and I had seen in the slurry wall and the bedrock. And I told them that down in the pit, I thought back to m family's arrival in New York Harbor, just offshore from here, and that the memory of looking up at the Statue of Liberty had inspired

---

[8] This is a fundamental defect which Libeskind saw in the other competing proposals that aimed to create an impressive high point, and ultimately to replace the Twin Towers.

part of my design. I envisioned five towers—tall but not too tall—arranged by increasing height, from south to north, so that they rose in a spiral with the same shape as the flame in Lady Liberty's torch. And the tallest, I had decided, should rise to 1,776 feet, to commemorate the Declaration of Independence, which brought democracy into the modern world. I would fill the upper floors of the tower with botanical gardens, as a confirmation of life (47).

In Libeskind's plan there is a memorial site going into the bedrock of Manhattan and exposing the foundations of the Twin Towers, and a walkway along the slurry wall. Sheltering the slurry wall in an embrace is a museum and other cultural buildings. In remembrance of the rescue workers, police, and firefighters, there is a map on which the routes taken by "the heroes of the day" to arrive at the towers are traced. These lines are incorporated into the design by turning them into pathways opening out into the city from a public space at the intersection of Fulton and Greenwich streets, which Libeskind calls "September 11 Plaza." There is also an even greater plaza, a triangular area that is proposed to become lower Manhattan's largest public space. Libeskind calls it "The Wedge of Light" which is inspired by the ray of sunlight. Indeed Libeskind attaches great importance to light, he says: "temples were venerated not just as architecture, but as gods in stone; lit up, they seemed filled with life, animated by ideas, ideals. Light is divine" (Libeskind, 2004 55). Further, the plaza is defined by two lines: the first is a line of light that strikes on September 11 of every year precisely at 8:46 a.m. –the moment when the first plane crashed into the North Tower. The second line marks the spot where, at 10:28 a.m., the moment the second tower fell. These two moments of September 11 defines "The Wedge of Light" that commemorates the events, united with another plaza called the "Park of Heroes." Libeskind offers a towering spire of 1,776 feet with gardens tied to a seventy-story skyscraper. Because gardens are "a constant affirmation of life" a skyscraper "rises above its predecessors, reasserting the pre-eminence of freedom and beauty, restoring the spiritual peak to the city, creating an icon that speaks of [American] vitality in the face of danger and [American] optimism in the aftermath of tragedy" (Libeskind, 2003). His conclusion to "World Center Design Study" reads: "Life victorious" (2003). Libeskind essentially appeals to the emotions of a traumatized public barely using an architectural term. In his choice of words he is more like a populist preacher than an architect in evoking the themes of memory and mourning, of commemoration and renewal, but what he skillfully achieves is a blurring of the distinction between commemoration and commercial development (Goldberger 213).

Ada Louis Huxtable writes in "Don't Blame the Architects" (June 7, 2003) in her column in *The Wall Street Journal* that Libeskind's plan "struck a common nerve:" "One had the sense, at the presentation, of an end to an undefined yearning and search. You could tell by the sustained applause and tears that this is what people really wanted, and what New York needs. [...] Forget the additional time and expense of a competition, nothing will ever be better than this" (www.online.wsj.com). Through the lens of the initial reactions to the plans for rebuilding Ground Zero it seems that the rebuilding efforts become something less than a commercial venture and a more symbolically political act, an opportunity to recreate the national fetish.

Libeskind's design is also important in that it "attains a perfect balance between aggression and desire" as the architecture critic of *The New York Times* Herbert Muschamp called it (quoted in Goldberger 137). In the design's phallic erectility aggression and desire meet. The phallus is a reactive, a defensive construct against the threat of castration. As the penetration of the hijacked jets into the Twin Towers on September 11 symbolically castrated them, the lost phallus, which was in fact never present, is doubly recreated with the erection of a taller tower on Ground Zero. Insofar as desire is the desire of the Other, of the Other's desire for recognition, in the re-erection of the tower an aggressive power play for domination and submission manifests itself. Here one can see the dialectic of mastery between the attacked (the so-called First World) and the attacker (the so-called Third World). However, as Hegelian dialectics show the master is only a master on the condition that the slave recognizes its power. Metaphorically, with September 11 attacks, the disadvantaged have recognized the existence of the powerful. With the erection of a taller tower, the powerful re-assert their dominance accompanied by their desire for recognition.

CONCLUSION

> It seems to me that the real political task in a society such as ours is to criticize the working of institutions which appear to be both neutral and independent; to criticize them in such a manner that the political violence which has always exercised itself obscurely through them will be unmasked, so that one can fight them.
>
> Michel Foucault, "Human Nature: Justice versus Power," 1974

This study of the American skyscraper offers a detailed critical inspection of the ways in which "the center of the center," the vertical *temenos* of The United States, New York City is construed as *the* place for the American Dream of material success with its overwhelming bundle of skyscrapers. The verticality offered by the Manhattan skyscrapers became an ideal, a paragon of American consumer and corporate culture. As The United States became a superpower in economic and political terms after World War II, it became the center of financial activity in the world, New York City being the core of this activity with its large and powerful financial institutions and bankers. Manhattan housing both these financial institutions and The United Nations Building is the heart of New York City. As New York became an ideal city, a model not only for The United States, but to the whole world as a world-class financial capital, it has been displaying its power through Manhattan's vertical space: the skyscrapers.

Space is a psychological, social, and an ideological product. Like any such product it has the capacity to hide consequences from those exposed to it. Because architecture is not just the product of a technical engineering process but is always socially and psychologically charged even though it seems neutral, how the built environment is created and organized offers ways of appropriating the workings of hierarchies and power relations in a society. Therefore architecture serves as the expression of psychological and social concerns of a society. Not only architecture is a manifestation of essential characteristics of a society but it also has the power to command and prohibit certain actions. Thus, the skyscraper form as an American invention reflects the characteristics of American society. As immediately observed in New York City's full flash of Manhattan skyline, the skyscraper in its grand form and towering height is an icon of economic and political power of the nation, an embodiment of the most distinctive American characteristic, of individualism.

When the skyscrapers were first built at the end of the nineteenth century they were regarded as the first original products, symbolic of a new civilization in the new world. They offered the expression of human energy and American individualism. Individualism refers to the main movement of liberal political and economic thought giving priority to individual interests rather than the group. The view that individuals have the ability to use their rationality according to their own desires and beliefs, and that they ought to be free civic agents is what defines individualism. This view portrays an individual who is an agent of free market liberalism and advocates a view of political and social liberty on these terms. As one of the most definitive elements of American culture, individualism is embedded in the idea of frontier of the American West as was famously formulated by Frederick Jackson Turner. However, the idea of the frontier is not limited to the West; it is ever changing, growing and evolving. Its progress is a "perennial rebirth," as Turner called it, for each time the frontier advances, the original encounter between civilization and wilderness is reproduced and the original challenges will be encountered once again. Just as once the West was the unknown, and was conquered and "Americanized" by the pioneers; the "new" frontier came with the skyscraper form in Manhattan where art (architecture) and finance (business) conquered the heavens. Patriotism and the rediscovery of the power of the frontier contributed to the creation of the skyscraper. Since the frontier ideal denies a history and claims self-reliant individualism, the skyscraper rose on the shoulders of those self-made individuals to claim the sky.

With the use of elevator, the steel frame, the development of fireproofing techniques, improved plumbing, heating and ventilation systems, and other technical improvements the skyscraper form evolved and the limitless possibility of building tall offered American businesspeople a new form of expressing their rise. Tall buildings became the architectural symbol of the economic world. The earliest skyscrapers developed out of the mercantile mentality, but they rose to prominence in the age of finance capitalism. The merchants who invested in tall buildings created the symbolism of size and height. Owners of the companies gave their names to the buildings, thereby establishing the association of verticality with wealth and power.

In their ever upward thrust skyscrapers mediate power, though masked, becoming an objectification of the ego ideal of the nation, that of being a winner in the competition to materialize the American Dream. In line with the ego ideal, the distinctive skyscraper in its style, location, or tallness also outpours aggression in dwarfing anything that has contact with it. If it was in the form of cathedrals and palaces that the church and the state speak and impose silence on the people, as Bataille argued in his "Architecture" (21), it is in the form of skyscrapers that architectural products inspire socially acceptable behavior and often fear through their tall erectility. A skyscraper speaks the language of the economically powerful, the ruling class and to assert the domination it is built extremely tall and large, one that cannot escape sight. In this respect skyscrapers follow the rationale for building large cathedrals to assert the smallness of the people before the rule of God. Only this time God becomes one of economic power, hence ideological coercion and political domination prevail.

Psychodynamics of space, the relationship between the subject, the society and the built environment reveals a complex web of discourses founded on the relationship not just between the individual and her/his internal world and external world but those between meaning, identity and power. This is a critically contingent field connecting the internal world (psyche) of the subject with the external world (the built environment) of a collection of subjects forming a society.

It is in this field that aggression takes on a more prominent role. Freud maintains that the more human beings control their aggressiveness the more intense will be their superegos' inclination to aggressiveness against their egos.

Libidinal instinctual impulses are repressed if they come into conflict with the subject's cultural and ethical ideas. Freud argues that the individual recognizes these ideas as a standard for himself and submits to the claims that they make on him (1914 93). Repression proceeds from the self-respect of the ego, in its attempts to avoid unpleasure.

The most important factor in this process is the formation of the ego ideal. The ego ideal, as an agency of the personality, results from the union of narcissism (idealization of the ego) and identification with the parents or with their substitutes, or with collective ideals. Not willing to leave the primary narcissism of childhood, in which the child is her/his own ideal, a substitute for that is created in the form of an ego ideal. Through idealization of the external object (the person her/himself, the leading person or idea, a person loved, or an object substituted for the loved one) ego ideal is formed; and members of the group are united by their relation to the external object besides their identification among themselves as equals before the illusion of love of the leader.

While the desires, conflicts, and needs of the individual in the group can be traced through her/his relationship to the external object, desires and conflicts within the urban space can be traced through its fabric, through the production of its specific space. In Manhattan urban space is immensely vertical with the skyscrapers' ever upward thrust. The vertical form is an ideal object through which New Yorkers and Americans are united. The skyscraper as an architectural product is a socially idealized object of American individualism.

The skyscraper form in its dominating presence in the urban fabric affects the psyche of the urban dweller. Since its creation during the end of nineteenth century, this dominating yet luring presence has been fascinating people through its magnetic, grand and tall shape, and has become an idealized external object. In this way it assumes a hypnotic role like that of the charismatic leader. In this object relationship the leader is spatially *above* the rest; those who are *under* its influence look *up* to it. Skyscrapers are phallic because they are built to stand erect, super tall and associated with power and wealth. It is in the skyscraper's phallic form and its being a "civic monument" to the ideal of individualism of the nation that its immense, yet hidden power emanates. Accordingly Lefebvre states: "monuments have a phallic aspect, *towers* exude arrogance, and the bureaucratic and political authoritarianism immanent to a repressive space is everywhere" (149). Insofar as a skyscraper assumes distinction in its location, style, and great height, that is insofar as it is a landmark in the urban fabric, it controls the subject's perception of spatial significations and more importantly created and maintained by the big money, it reproduces the value systems of the powerful. As all buildings are marked by the production of spaces of domination, the skyscraper disguised as a civic monument condenses the diffuse power relations into a particular site. Although monumental buildings hide, legitimize or help subjects internalize power relations, they transmit their message clearly, making the quality of that space closed to alternative readings, and by doing so, they ultimately draw the subjects into an illusion that the values they represent are common and shared among the society. Spaces are never empty, and the content for monumental space is "designed to conceal: namely, the phallic realm of (supposed) virility. It is at the same time an aggressive and repressive space: nothing in it escapes the surveillance of power" (Lefebvre 147). From this point, skyscrapers as monumental buildings function like the phallus since they make visible and "look back" to the subject in the street, reproducing repressive spaces which both celebrate entrepreneurship and individualism while unleashing their aggressiveness, threatening to cast out (castrate) the ones who are doubtful of the celebration. This violently castrating space "isolates the phallus, projecting it into a realm outside the body, then fixes it in space (verticality) and brings it under the surveillance of the eye [...] because of the process of localization, because of the fragmentation and specialization of space" (Lefebvre 310).

The built environment acts as a mediator of power. It mediates, constructs and reproduces power relations. However silent, architectural products control the individual in her/his dwelling places, as her/his action is both structured and shaped by walls, doors, and windows. Like the horizontal wall in Kafka's story, this vertical form protects and keeps those who are exposed to its display of power in union. Though this aggression is mainly towards the "other," insiders are not exempt from it. Because the skyscraper is an American invention and it is most often associated with The United States than anywhere else in the world, the subject through her/his narcissistic idealization of the perceived common ideal of the American Dream of material success see in it her/his own ideals, a place where s/he herself/himself wants to be, reasoning under the influence of the superego. In this mechanism the ideal –like the symbolic father- works in a covert aggression and threat forcing the subject to internalize the law of individualism on the way up the social and economic ladder if s/he does not want to be castrated in the society. It is through the imposition of the vertical architectonics of skyscrapers that their phallic power unleashes aggressiveness, which is central to the narcissistic workings of the superego. This violently castrating urban space is essentially aggressive; a site of disintegration, dissolution, and alienation for the subject.

In the vertical built environment the scopic drive dominates diffuse power relations in the urban fabric. The subject is not the only one that is driven by the urge to look, but the architectural product also "looks back" through the gaze. Because the space, the built environment is not fixed, but is dynamic in a dialectical relationship with the subject, it shows and hides, protects and threatens, unites and separates, and provides ways of understanding the interaction between space, identity and power. Specifically, distinctive skyscrapers such as the Twin Towers of the World Trade Center, and their predecessor the Freedom Tower cannot escape the visual field thereby mediating power in their phallic form.

Architectural products, the built environment is necessarily shaped according to certain interests in quest of profit, status, power, or aesthetics. However, the built environment is taken as a given; it is taken for granted most of the time, and this unquestioned, silent nature is the very key to its complex relations with power.

Disciplinary power transforms human beings into subjects through micro-practices. The most important of these micro-practices is the *gaze*. Within spatial relations a normalizing regime is established and the gaze of surveillance controls deviations from it. The fiction of a never ending, permanent gaze from the central tower is what makes the subjects docile to the workings of the system at large. A similar process of dispersal of power relations through the impersonal gaze emanates from the distinctive, "central" corporate towers, with a significant difference. In the heart of New York City, Manhattan, the vertical urban fabric does not allow a reliance on a single power (the central tower) but a multiplicity of central towers. Spatial domination through grand size or dominant location is able to dwarf the human subject securing compliance to the rules of the financial game as it points to the power necessary for its reproduction. This is not an overt kind of power one can observe in spatial constructs such as fortresses, but a hidden and silent one operating through the compliance of the subject to surveillance.

Each distinctive, landmark skyscraper becomes a mediator of a disciplinary process with its corporate imagery and symbolism of big money intimidating and threatening to cast out those who cannot fight well enough to win for themselves an office space in the higher ground, or a *high* ranking position anywhere as failures. Therefore without ever having to resort to physical violence, a "symbolic violence" is unleashed. Silence and masking; violence passing itself off as legitimate are definitive of symbolic violence. This symbolic violence embedded in the workings of symbolic capital significantly operates within the field of vision. It needs to be exhibited to such a great degree so as to be seen by others. It is in the voyeurism and exhibitionism of the skyscraper with its largeness and tallness that cannot escape the gaze of observers, lies its symbolic power. The aura that the skyscraper generates is its symbolic capital. Although growing tallness is not an element that increases the skyscraper's efficiency, each and every day a new project for "the tallest building in the world" makes its way to the headlines. It is the image, the symbolic capital of a skyscraper that will distinguish it from other skyscrapers and give it a market advantage for rental: The successful corporate tower offers a distinctive image to which lessees are invited to link their corporate image. Distinction is also achieved through a quest for uniqueness of form whether viewed in the city skyline or in relation to neighboring buildings. If a building leaves a mark on the land it becomes monumental. If it becomes monumental, it has more ability to exert more symbolic violence. Being monuments to economic success, Manhattan skyscrapers "watch" not only the nation, but the globe at large, transferring the necessary and intimidating power relations of global capitalism. However, their "silent" surveillance is dangerous, since the insidiousness of the gaze translates itself into a form of symbolic violence, robbing the observers off their capability to see the workings of such power dispersal.

Foucault underlines the ever shifting disguises of power, arguing it is essential for power relations to be reproduced they should be hidden and masked (1980 86). As was exemplified by Foucault in *Discipline and Punish* through the panopticon, architecture functions as an agent of the aims and techniques of the government of societies. He writes that the major effect of the panopticon -where the effects of surveillance is permanent, even if it is not so in its action- is to make the inmate to think that s/he is being watched all the time, assuring an automatic functioning of power (1975 201). Visibility assumes a great role in this function, where it is organized entirely around the idea of an "all-seeing power." This is a mode of operation through which power will be exercised through the things being known and people seen in an immediate, collective and anonymous gaze. Surveillance is achieved through the normalizing gaze, which in turn makes the subjects internalize power. Foucault contends that in the system of surveillance all that is needed is the idea of a panoptic gaze turning the subjects overseers of themselves (1980 155).

Spatial domination also seduces, or manipulates the desires of the subject ranging from self-annihilation to self-preservation depending on the subject's notion of self identity. This underlines the fact that spatial constructs shape the subject's perception of both her/himself and others. Because distinctive skyscrapers inherently carry the economic power, and the resultant political authority of the corporation or corporations for which they are logos and symbols, the subject feels the urge to share in that power affirming and legitimizing the very authority s/he is put under as s/he participates in its dominance.

Symbolic violence imposes systems of symbolism and meaning upon groups or classes in such a way that they are experienced as legitimate (Jenkins 104). It is this legitimacy that obscures power relations which allow that imposition to be successful. As long as it is perceived as legitimate, culture adds its own force to those power relations, contributing to their systematic reproduction. Cultural reproduction contributes to maintaining the power of dominant groups. Significantly this is achieved through *misrecognition* (mèconnaissance): "the process whereby power relations are perceived not for what they objectively are but in a form which renders them legitimate in the eyes of the beholder" (Bourdieu and Passeron xiii).

It is through the largeness and tallness, the symbolic power of the skyscrapers that people come to be exposed to symbolic violence in the American context, most effective in New York City's Manhattan. Skyscrapers were responses to market pressure for more rentable space on a given site area; however the physical limits to the increase in site efficiency is cut back by the fact that the skyscraper reaches a point where the cost of increased height exceeds the gains in rental area (Dovey 107). Given the functional inefficiencies, it would be expected that the race for the tallest skyscraper would slow down, but it does not. The proliferation of corporate skyscrapers then depends not on a functional reason but a symbolic one: that of "symbolic capital" in Bourdieu's terms.

Bourdieu sees power as diffuse or symbolic which is often masked, regarding this symbolic power intertwined with economic and political power thereby serving a legitimating function. Individuals and groups draw upon a variety of cultural, social, and symbolic resources in order to maintain and enhance their positions in the social order. Bourdieu conceptualizes such resources as capital when they function as a "social relation of power," that is when they become objects of struggle as valued resources. Symbolic capital is the value that can be attributed to a symbolic, aesthetic or mythological "aura." It is a form of power that is exercised through "an action of knowledge" which "enables one to account for the relations of force that are actualized in and by relations of cognition (or recognition) and of communication" (Bourdieu, 1999 336). For Bourdieu, the logic of the symbolic is fundamentally diacritical (distinguishing), and distinction is the specific form of profit that symbolic capital procures: Symbolic capital is there for the gaze of others, and it is in this exhibition distinction is achieved.

It is in the skyscraper's exhibition of corporate power and wealth that they draw the subject's desire to look. In "Three Essays on Sexuality" Freud argues that "visual impressions remain the most frequent pathway along which libidinal excitation is aroused" (69). Pleasure in looking becomes a perversion, according to Freud, in the form of voyeurism and its double exhibitionism: "anyone who is an exhibitionist in his unconscious is at the same time a *voyeur*" (81). Freud's formulation as reworked by Lacan in the split between the organic eye and the gaze takes on a significant plane in respect to towers. The towers with their soaring height incorporate a panoptic view of the city, gazing back at the walking subject. The gaze on part of the tower is aggressive since it belittles the one on the street, hence pouring out symbolic violence. This process is further underlined by Freud's assertion that the force which opposes "scopophilia" is shame (1905 69). The towers of Manhattan are also voyeurs gazing back at the subject and exhibitionists in their "unashamed" display of power. This becomes more forceful in the case of the World Trade Center as the peak of the vertical city, and as "the most monumental figure of Western urban development" (de Certeau 93).

Underlining the monumental aspect the Twin Towers reached a hundred and ten stories replacing the Empire State Building as the tallest. Indeed, after their completion in 1972 and 1973 the Twin Towers became the world's tallest buildings, only to be replaced by Chicago's Sears Tower a year later. Although they were no longer the world's tallest, they were the world's largest in terms of rentable office space until their destruction. They stood taller than any other skyscraper in New York's skyline and conveyed a symbolic message of American Dream of material success and achievement. They stood as a symbol of America's financial power and as a symbol of American culture. After their destruction the Twin Towers came to represent destruction and terror in a city traumatized by the unprecedented attacks of September 11, 2001.

A border between patriot and enemy was already drawn immediately after the attacks by the American government. The American government construed the attacks as attacks on "freedom," on "American values," on the "American way of life." According to the official narrative it was the "American culture" that was attacked. Then in the light of the official rhetoric, American culture, as symbolized by the Twin Towers, is one of neo-liberal global capitalism. As nothing seems to be weakening the "anonymous centers" of deterritorialized global capitalism, fallen Twin Towers are being replaced by even higher towers. Indeed as Žižek writes, the real politico-ideological catastrophe of September 11 was not that of the U.S., on the contrary: "the result of September 11 is an unprecedented strengthening of American hegemony, in all its aspects" (2002 144). It is clearly seen in the unique doubleness of the Twin Towers before their fall in September 11 and the symbolism inherent in the master plan for rebuilding the site where Twin Towers once stood.

The study at hand reads architecture and the rebuilding plan for Ground Zero as a political act, because "The World Trade Center was the eye of a needle through which global capital flowed, the seat of an empire. However anonymous they appeared, the Twin Towers were never benign, never just architecture. Recovering this site for the living city is, therefore, inescapably political" (Sorkin and Zukin xi). Further, "War and destruction were the constituent elements of the act of making order out of chaos in the histories of creation. Building skyscrapers as an act of violence is the primordial act of establishing order in the built environment" (Van Leeuwen 54). Indeed, building an even taller skyscraper dubbed as Freedom Tower in place of the fallen ones, The United States responds violently to an act of violence.

In the "Design Plan for Freedom Tower" architect Daniel Libeskind assures the agency in charge of rebuilding Ground Zero, LMDC, that the new tower will become a "lasting icon and a symbol of renewal" to "recapture the skyline and establish a new civic icon for this city and our country" (www.renewnyc.org). "The impulse to rebuild instantly captured the public imagination as an opportunity to express the resolve of the nation. Ground Zero, in other words, is already an ideologically charged site (Ross 127). Indeed in its report "A Vision for Lower Manhattan" (2002), LMDC sets out the very ideology of the rebuilding the tower: The design should serve the goal to underline the status of New York City as the destination of a pagan pilgrimage, as the destination of a quest for material success. Hence LMDC's chosen plan, which "preserves and reveals the slurry walls of the bathtub of the

World Trade Center site as a symbol and physical embodiment of the resilience of American democracy and freedom in withstanding the attacks of September 11th 2001" (www.renewnyc.org) is another architectural venture to rebuild the lost object of mourning in the form of an ego ideal in New York City.

The guiding idea for Libeskind's plan for rebuilding Ground Zero, which he calls "The Memory Foundations," is a new architecture based on "democratic ideals" (43) embodied in his childhood remembrance of the Statue of Liberty. Freedom Tower is 1,776 feet tall, to commemorate the Declaration of Independence, stands in a way to salute the Statue of Liberty, underlining the architect's idea that it is in the form of architecture which people keep their faith in democracy exemplary of the modern world.

Libeskind's design is also important in that it "attains a perfect balance between aggression and desire" as the architecture critic of *The New York Times* Herbert Muschamp called it (quoted in Goldberger 137). In the design's phallic erectility where aggression and desire meet. The phallus is a reactive, a defensive construct against the threat of castration. As the penetration of the hijacked jets into the Twin Towers on September 11 symbolically castrated them, the lost phallus, which was in fact never present, is doubly recreated with the erection of a taller tower on Ground Zero. Insofar as desire is the desire of the Other, of the Other's desire for recognition, in the re-erection of the tower an aggressive power play for domination and submission manifests itself. Here one can see the dialectic of mastery between the attacked (the so-called First World) and the attacker (the so-called Third World). However, as Hegelian dialectics show the master is only a master on the condition that the slave recognizes its power. Metaphorically, with September 11 attacks, the disadvantaged have recognized the existence of the powerful. With the erection of a taller tower, the powerful re-assert their dominance accompanied by their desire for recognition, once again underlining it *is* New York City that will remain as the seat of omnipotent power relations.

BIBLIOGRAPHY

Adams, Thomas. et al. *The Building of the City, The Regional Plan of New York and Its Environs.* Vol. 2. New York, 1931.

Adorno, Theodor. "Sociology and Psychology I." 1967. *New Left Review* 46 (November-December 1967): 67-80.

----------. "Sociology and Psychology II." 1968. *New Left Review* 47 (January-February 1968): 79-97.

----------. "Functionalism Today." In *Rethinking Architecture: A Reader in Cultural Theory.* Ed. Neil Leach. London and New York: Routledge, 1997. pp. 6-19.

Althusser, Louis. *Lenin and Philosophy and Other Essays.* Trans. Ben Brewster. London: New Left, 1971.

Barth, Gunther. *City People.* New York: Oxford University Press, 1980.

Barthes, Roland. *The Pleasure of the Text.* 1973. Trans. Richard Miller. New York: Farrar, Strauss and Giroux, 1975.

----------. *The Eiffel Tower and Other Mythologies.* 1979. Trans. Richard Howard. Berkeley: The University Press of California, 1997.

Bataille, George. "Architecture." In *Rethinking Architecture: A Reader in Cultural Theory.* Ed. Neil Leach. London and New York: Routledge, 1997. p. 21.

Batur, Enis. "Joyce'un Kulesi." [The Tower of Joyce]. Preface to *Ulysses.* James Joyce. Trans. Nevzat Erkmen. Istanbul: YKY, 1996.

Baudrillard, Jean. *Amerika.* 1986. Trans. Yaşar Avunç. İstanbul: Ayrıntı Yayınları, 1996.

----------. *Simulations.* Trans. P. Foss, P. Patton, and P. Beitchman. New York: Semiotext(e): 1983.

Benedetto, Richard and Jill Lawrence. "Candidates Bash Each Other on Iraq, Terrorism." *USA Today.* October 19, 2004. p. 8A.

Berman, Marshall. *All That Is Solid Melts into Air: The Experience of Modernity.* New York: Simon and Schuster, 1982.

Bierce, Ambrose. *The Devil's Dictionary: A Guide Book for Cynics.* 1906. San Diego: The Book Tree, 2000.

Bletter, Rosemarie Haag. "The Invention of the Skyscraper: Notes on its Diverse Histories." *Assemblege 2* (February 1987):110-117.

Bourdieu, Pierre. "Intellectual Field and Creative Project." In *Knowledge and Control: New Directions for Sociology of Education.* Ed. Michael K. D. Young. London: Collier Macmillan, 1971. pp. 161-188.

----------. and Jean-Claude Passeron. *Reproduction in Education, Society and Culture.* 1970. Trans. Richard Nice. London and Beverly Hills: Sage Publications, 1977.

----------. *The Logic of Practice.* 1970. Trans. Richard Nice. Cambridge: Polity Press, 1992.

----------. *Outline of a Theory of Practice.* 1972. Trans. Richard Nice. Cambridge: Cambridge University Press, 2005.

----------. *Distinction: A Social Critique of the Judgement of Taste.* 1979. Trans. Richard Nice. Cambridge: Harvard University Press, 2002.

----------. "Forms of Capital." In *Handbook of Theory and Research for the Sociology of Education*. Ed. J. G. Richardson. New York: Greenwood Press, 1986. pp. 241-258.

----------. *In Other Words: Essays towards a Reflexive Sociology*. 1986. Stanford: Stanford University Press, 1990.

----------. et al. *The Weight of the World: Social Suffering in Contemporary Society*. Trans. Priscilla Parkhurst Ferguson et al. Stanford: Stanford University Press, 1999.

----------. "Scattered Remarks." Trans. Tarik Wareh and Loïc Wacquant. *European Journal of Social Theory* 2:3 (1999): 334-340.

Brunner, José. *Freud and the Politics of Psychoanalysis*. Cambridge: Blackwell, 1995.

Boyer, M. Christine. *The City of Collective Memory: Its Historical Imagery and Architectural Entertainments*. Cambridge: MIT Press, 1996.

Burrows, Edwin D. and Mike Wallace. Eds. *Gotham: A History of New York City to 1898*. New York: Oxford University Press, 1999.

Butler, Judith. *Precarious Life: The Powers of Mourning and Violence*. London and New York: Verso, 2004.

Calvino, Italo. Invisible Cities. 1972. Trans. W. Weaver. New York: Harcourt Brace & Company, 1974.

Cantwell, Anne-Marie and Diana diZerega Wall. *Unearthing Gotham: The Archeology of New York City*. New Haven and London: Yale University Press, 2001.

CNN. Official Website. Accessed 21 February 2004.
<http:www.cnstudentnews.cnn.com/TRANSCRIPTS/0207/16/wbr.00.html>

Condit, Carl W. *The Rise of the Skyscraper*. Chicago: University of Chicago Press, 1952.

Dali, Salvador. "New York Salutes Me!" Spain, May 23, 1941.

Davis, Richard Harding. "Broadway." *Scribner's*. 15 (1891): 588-560.

De Certeau, Michel. *The Practice of Everyday Life*. Trans. Steven Rendall. Berkeley: University of California Press, 1984.

Dieter, Arnold. *Building in Egypt: Pharaonic Stone Masonry*. New York: Oxford University Press, 1997.

Dos Passos, John. *Manhattan Transfer*. 1925. London: Penguin Books, 2000.

Dovey, Kim. *Framing Places: Mediating Power in Built Form*. London and New York: Routledge, 1999.

Eagleton, Terry. *Ideology: An Introduction*. 1991. London: Verso, 2000.

Eliot, T. S. "Tradition and the Individual Talent." 1919. In *The Norton Anthology of Theory and Criticism*. Gen. Ed. Vincent B. Leitch. New York: W.W. Norton and Company, 2001. pp. 1092-1098.

----------. *The Waste Land*. 1922. New York: Dover Publications, 1998.

Eribon, Didier. *Michel Foucault*. Trans. Betsy Wing. Cambridge: Harvard University Press, 1991.

Evans, Dylan. *An Introductory Dictionary of Lacanian Psychoanalysis*. New York: Routledge, 1996.

Ferree, Barr. "The High Building and Its Art." *Scribner's*. 38 (1894): 297-

Fitzgerald, F. Scott. *The Great Gatsby*. 1926. London: Penguin Books, 1990.

----------. "My Lost City." 1936. In *Empire City: New York Through the Centuries*. Eds. Kenneth T. Jackson and David S. Dunbar. New York: Columbia University Press, 2002. pp.602-610.

Forgey, Benjamin. "Buildings that Stood Tall as Symbols of Strength." Accessed 4 June 2003 <http://www.washingtonpost.com/ac2/wpdyn?pagename=article&node=&contentld=A212>

Foucault, Michel. "A Preface to Transgression." 1963a. In *Language, Counter-Memory, Practice: Selected Essays and Interviews by Michel Foucault*. 1977. Ed. Donald Bouchard. Trans. Sherry Simon. New York: Cornell University Press, 1988. pp.29-52.

----------. *Birth of the Clinic: An Archeology of Medical Perception*. 1963b. New York: Vintage, 1994.

----------. *The Order of Things: An Archeology of the Human Sciences*. 1966. New York: Vintage Books, 1994.

----------. *Discipline and Punish: The Birth of the Prison*. 1975. Trans. Alan Sheridan. New York: Vintage Books, 1995.

----------. *Power/Knowledge: Selected Interviews and Other Writings 1972-1977*. Ed. Colin Gordon. New York: Pantheon Books, 1980.

----------. *The Foucault Reader*. Ed. Paul Rabinow. New York: Pantheon Books, 1984.

----------. "Of Other Spaces: Utopias and Heterotopias." In *Rethinking Architecture: A Reader in Cultural Theory*. Ed. Neil Leach. London and New York: Routledge, 1997. pp. 348-356.

The Fountain Head. 1949. Dir. King Vidor. Warner. 114 mins.

Fourny, Jean-François. "Bourdieu's Uneasy Psychoanalysis." Trans. Meaghan Emery. *SubStance* 29:3 (2000): 103-112.

Freud, Sigmund. "Three Essays on the Theory of Sexuality." 1905. In *On Sexuality: Three Essays on the Theory of Sexuality and Other Works*. The Pelican Freud Library Vol. 7. Trans. James Strachey. Gen. Ed. Angela Richards. New York: Penguin Books, 1977. pp. 33-170.

----------. *Totem and Taboo.* 1913. The Standard Edition. Trans. James Strachey. New York: W. W. Norton & Company, 1989.

----------. "On Narcissism: An Introduction." 1914. In *The Standard Edition of the Complete Psychological Works of Sigmund Freud: On the History of the Psycho-Analytic Movement; Papers on Metapsychology and Other Works*. Vol. XIV. Ed. and Trans. James Strachey. London: The Hogarth Press and the Institute of Psychoanalysis, 1953. pp. 73-102.

----------. "Mourning and Melancholia." 1917. In *The Standard Edition of the Complete Psychological Works of Sigmund Freud: On the History of the Psycho-Analytic Movement; Papers on Metapsychology and Other Works*. Vol. XIV. Ed. and Trans. James Strachey. London: The Hogarth Press and the Institute of Psychoanalysis, 1953. pp. 239-258.

----------. "The 'Uncanny'." 1919. Trans. Alix Strachey. In *The Norton Anthology of Theory and Criticism*. Gen. Ed. Vincent B. Leitch. New York: W. W. Norton & Company, 2001. pp. 929-952.

----------. *Beyond the Pleasure Principle.* 1920. The Standard Edition. Trans. James Strachey. New York: W. W. Norton & Company, 1989.

----------. *Group Psychology and the Analysis of the Ego.* 1921. The

Standard Edition. Trans. James Strachey. New York: W. W. Norton & Company, 1989.

----------. *The Ego and the Id*. 1923. The Standard Edition. Trans. James Strachey. New York: W. W. Norton & Company, 1989.

----------. "Fetishism." 1927. Trans. Joan Rivière. In *The Norton Anthology of Theory and Criticism*. Gen. Ed. Vincent B. Leitch. New York: W. W. Norton & Company, 2001. pp. 952-956.

----------. *Civilization and Its Discontents*. 1930. The Standard Edition. Trans. James Strachey. New York: W. W. Norton & Company, 1989.

Giedion, Siegfried. *Space, Time and Architecture*. Cambridge: Harvard University Press, 1967.

Glanz, James and Eric Lipton. *City in the Sky: The Rise and Fall of the World Trade Center*. New York: Times Books Henry Holt and Company, 2003.

Goldberger, Paul. *Up from Zero: Politics, Architecture, and the Rebuilding of New York*. New York: Random House, 2005.

Gottmann, Jean. "Why the Skyscraper?" *The Geographical Review*. 56:2 (April 1966): 190-212.

Hammack, David. *Power and Society: Greater New York at the Turn of the Century*. New York: Russell Sage Foundation, 1982.

Harvey, David. *The Condition of Postmodernity*. Cambridge: Blackwell, 1990.

Howells, William Dean. *A Hazard of New Fortunes*. 1889. London: Penguin, 2001.

The Hudsucker Proxy. 1994. Dir. Joel Coen. Warner Bros. 111 mins.

Huxtable, Ada Louise. *The Tall Building Artistically Reconsidered: The Search for a Skyscraper Style.* New York: Pantheon Books, 1984.

----------. "Don't Blame the Architects: The WTC Designs Are Visionary, but Process Is Business as Usual." *The Wall Street Journal.* January 7, 2003. Accessed 25 October 2005. <http://www.online.wsj.com>

Irving, Washington. *Knickerbocker's History of New York.* 1809. New York: IndyPublish, 2006.

Isaac, Jeffrey C. "Beyond the Three Faces of Power: A Realist Critique." In *Rethinking Power.* Ed. Thomas E. Wartenberg. Albany: SUNY Press, 1992. pp. 32-55.

Jacobs, Jane. *The Death and Life of Great American Cities.* 1961. New York: Vintage Books, 1992.

Jackson, Kenneth T. and David S. Dunbar. Eds. *Empire City: New York Through the Centuries.* New York: Columbia University Press, 2002.

James, Henry. *The American Scene.* 1907. In *Collected Travel Writings, Great Britain and America: English Hours, The American Scene, Other Travels.* New York: The Library of America, 1993. pp.351-736.

Jameson, Fredric. "Imaginary and Symbolic in Lacan: Marxism, Psychoanalytic Criticism, and the Problem of the Subject." In *Literature and Psychoanalysis: The Question of Reading: Otherwise.* Ed. Shoshana Felman. Baltimore: Johns Hopkins University Press, 1982. 338-397.

Jenkins, Richard. *Pierre Bourdieu.* Revised Ed. Key Sociologists Series. Ed. Peter Hamilton. London and New York: Routledge, 2002.

Kafka, Franz. "The Great Wall of China." In *The Penguin Complete Stories of Franz Kafka*. Ed. Nahum N. Glatzer. London: Penguin, 1983. pp. 235-248.

Kasinitz, Philip. Ed. *Metropolis: Centre and Symbol of Our Times*. London: Macmillan, 1995.

Keller, Morton. *The Life Insurance Enterprise: 1885-1910*. Cambridge: Harvard University Press, 1963.

King Kong. 2005. Dir. Peter Jackson. Universal Pictures. 179 mins.

King's Handbook of New York City. Boston: Moses King, 1893.

Koolhaas, Rem. *Delirious New York: A Retroactive Manifesto for Manhattan*. 1978. New York: The Monacelli Press, 1994.

Kracauer, Siegfried. "On Employment Agencies: The Construction of a Space." Trans. David Frisby. In *Rethinking Architecture: A Reader in Cultural Theory*. Ed. Neil Leach. London and New York: Routledge, 1997. pp. 59-64.

Lacan, Jacques. "The Mirror Stage as Formative of the *I* Function." 1949. In *Écrits: A Selection*. Trans. Bruce Fink. New York and London: Norton, 2004. pp. 1-9.

----------. "The Function of Speech and Language in Psychoanalysis." 1953. In *Écrits: A Selection*. Trans. Bruce Fink. New York and London: Norton, 2004. pp.31-106.

----------. "The Freudian Thing, or the Meaning of the Return to Freud in Psychoanalysis." 1955. In *Écrits: A Selection*. Trans. Bruce Fink. New York and London: Norton, 2004. pp.107-137.

----------. "The Signification of the Phallus." 1958. In *Écrits: A Selection*. Trans. Bruce Fink. New York and London: Norton, 2004. pp.271-280.

----------. "The Subversion of the Subject and the Dialectic of Desire in the Freudian Unconscious." 1960. In *Écrits: A Selection*. Trans. Bruce Fink. New York and London: Norton, 2004. pp. 281-312.

----------. *The Four Fundamental Concepts of Psychoanalysis*. 1973. The Seminar of Jacques Lacan Book XI. Ed. Jacques-Alain Miller. Trans. Alan Sheridan. New York and London: Norton, 1998.

----------. "A Theoretical Introduction to the Functions of Psychoanalysis in Criminology." Trans. M. Bracher et al. *Journal for the Psychoanalysis of Culture and Society* 1:2 (1996): 13-25.

Laplanche J. and J.-B. Pontalis. *The Lanugage of Psycho-Analysis*. 1967. Trans. Donald Nicholson-Smith. New York and London: W.W. Norton & Company, 1973.

Lasch, Christopher. "The Freudian Left and Cultural Revolution." *New Left Review* 129 (Sept.-Oct. 1981): 23-34.

Leach, Neil. Ed. "Introduction." *Rethinking Architecture: A Reader in Cultural Theory*. London and New York: Routledge, 1997.

Le Corbusier. *The Radiant City*. Trans. Pamela Knight, Eleanor Levieux, and Derek Coltman. New York: The Orion Press, 1967.

----------. "The Fairy Catastrophe." 1936. In *Empire City: New York Through the Centuries*. Eds. Kenneth T. Jackson and David S. Dunbar. New York: Columbia University Press, 2002. pp.611-618.

Leeuwen, Thomas A. P. *The Skyward Trend of Thought: The Metaphysics of the American Skyscraper*. Cambridge: MIT Press, 1988.

Lefebvre, Henri. *The Production of Space*. 1974. Trans. Donald Nicholson Smith. Malden: Blackwell Publishing, 1991.

LeGates, Richard T. and Frederic Stout. *The City Reader*. 3rd Ed. London and New York: Routledge, 2003.

Libeskind, Daniel. *Breaking Ground*. New York: Riverhead Books, 2004.

----------. Official Web Site. "World Trade Center Design Study." 2003. Accessed 2 June 2004. <http://www.daniel-libeskind.com/press/index.html>

----------. "Design Plan for Freedom Tower." Accessed 21 February 2004. <www.renewnyc.org/plan_des_dev/wtc-site/new_design_plans/freedom_tower_dec_19.asp>

LMDC. Lower Manhattan Development Corporation Official Website. Accessed 21 February 2004. <http:www.renewnyc.org>

Ludington, Townsend. *John Dos Passos: A Twentieth Century Odyssey*. New York: Dutton, 1980.

Lynch, Kevin. *Image of the City*. Cambridge: MIT Press, 1960.

Marx, Karl and Friedrich Engels. *The Communist Manifesto*. 1848. Trans. Samuel Moore. London: Penguin Books, 2002.

McCabe Jr., James D. *Light and Shadows of New York Life*. 1872. New York: Farrar, Strauss and Giroux, 1970.

Mitchell, Juliet. *Psychoanalysis and Feminism: Freud, Reich, Laing, and Women*. New York: Pantheon Books, 1974.

Mumford, Lewis. "Skyscrapers and Tenements." 1933. In *The Sidewalk Critic: Lewis Mumford's Writings on New York*. Ed. Robert

Wojtowicz. New York: Princeton Architectural Press, 1998. pp. 100-102.

----------. *Sticks and Stones: A Study of American Architecture and Civilization.* New York: Norton, 1934a.

----------. "Modern Design and The New Bryant Park." 1934b. In *The Sidewalk Critic: Lewis Mumford's Writings on New York.* Ed. Robert Wojtowicz. New York: Princeton Architectural Press, 1998. pp. 121-124.

----------. "What is a City?" 1937. In *The City Reader.* 3rd Ed. Eds. Richard T. LeGates and Frederic Stout. London and New York: Routledge, 2003. pp. 93-96.

----------. Ed. *Roots of Contemporary American Architecture.* 1952. New York: Dover Publications, 1972.

----------. *The Brown Decades: A Study of the Arts in America 1865-1895.* New York: Dover, 1959.

Nalbantoğlu, Gülsüm Baydar. "Project(ion)s." *Assemblage* 41 (April 2000): 58.

New York Guide. American Guide Series. New York: Random House, 1935.

O. Henry. "Psyche and the Skyscraper." In *Strictly Business: More Stories from the Four Million.* New York: BiblioBazaar, 2006. pp. 112-117.

Ricoeur, Paul. *History and Truth.* Evanston: Northwestern University Press, 1965.

Ross, Andrew. "The Odor of Publicity." In *After the World Trade Center: Rethinking New York City.* Eds. Michael Sorkin and Sharon Zukin. New York: Routledge, 2002. pp.121-130.

Rubin, Barbara. "Ideology and Urban Design." *AAAG* 69 (September 1979): 339-361.

Sanders, James. *Celluloid Skyline: New York and the Movies*. New York: Alfred A. Knopf, 2003.

Sartre, Jean Paul. "New York, the Colonial City." In *Literary and Philosophical Essays*. New York: Collier Books, 1970. pp. 126-132.

Scarry, Elaine. "Acts of Resistance." *Harper's* (May 2004): 15-20.

Schuyler, Montgomery. "The Skyscraper Problem." *Scribner's* 34 (1903): 253-256.

Shultz, Earle and Walter Simmons. *Offices in the Sky*. Indianapolis: Bobbs-Merrill, 1959.

Simmel, Georg. "The Metropolis and Mental Life." 1903. Trans. Edward Shills. In *Metropolis: Centre and Symbol of Our Times*. Ed. Philip Kasinitz. London: Macmillan, 1995. pp. 30-45.

Simonson, Harold P. Ed. "Introduction" to *The Significance of The Frontier in American History*. 1893. Frederick Jackson Turner. New York: Frederick Ungar Publishing Co., 1979.

Sorkin, Michael and Sharon Zukin. Eds. *After the World Trade Center: Rethinking New York City*. New York: Routledge, 2002.

Spann, Edward. *The New Metropolis*. New York: Columbia University Press, 1981.

Starrett, Col. W. A. "The First Skyscraper."1928. In *Roots of Contemporary American Architecture*. Ed. Lewis Mumford. New York: Dover Publications, 1972. pp.237-242.

Stern, Robert A.M., Gregory Gilmartin and Thomas Mellins. *New York 1930: Architecture and Urbanism between the Two World Wars*. New York: Rizzoli, 1987.

Strauss, Anselm. *Images of the American City*. New York: The Free Press, 1961.

Sullivan, Henry Louis. "The Tall Office Building Artistically Considered." *Lippincott's Magazine*. 57 (1896): 403-409. Reprinted in *An American Primer*. Ed. Daniel Boarstin. Chicago: University of Chicago Press, 1969. pp. 562-570.

Swartz, David. *Culture and Power: The Sociology of Pierre Bourdieu*. Chicago: The University of Chicago Press, 1997.

Turner, Frederick Jackson. *The Significance of the Frontier in American History*. 1893. New York: Frederick Ungar Publishing Co., 1979.

Vanderwerken, David L. "Manhattan Transfer: Dos Passos' Babel Story." *American Literature* 49:2 (May 1977): 253-267.

Van Dyke, John C. *The New New York*. New York: Macmillan, 1999.

Vidler, Anthony. *The Architectural Uncanny: Essays in the Modern Unhomely*. Cambridge: The MIT Press, 1992.

Webster, J. Carson. "The Skyscraper: Logical and Historical Considerations." *Journal of the Society of Architectural Historians*. 17:4 (December 1959): 126-139.

Weisman, Winston. "New York and the Problem of the First Skyscraper." *Journal of the Society of Architectural Historians*. 12:1 (March 1953): 13-21.

----------. "A New View of Skyscraper History." In *The Rise of an American Architecture*. Ed. Edgar Kaufmann, Jr. New York: Praeger, 1970. pp. 115-160.

White, E. B. *Here is New York.* 1949. New York: The Little Bookroom, 1999.

"The White House." "Address to a Joint Session of Congress and the American People." September 20, 2001. Accessed 3 April 2005. <http://whitehouse.gov/news/releases/2001/10/20011010-3.html.>

Whitman, Walt. "Manhatta." 1860. In *Empire City: New York Through the Centuries*. Eds. Kenneth T. Jackson and David S. Dunbar. New York: Columbia University Press, 2002. p. 253.

Williams, Raymond. *The Country and the City.* 1973. New York: Oxford University Press, 1975.

Willis, Carol. *Form Follows Finance: Skyscrapers and Skylines in New York and Chicago.* New York: Princeton Architectural Press, 1995.

Working Girl. 1988. Dir. Mike Nichols. 20th Century-Fox. 115 mins.

Zaretsky, Eli. "Bisexuality, Capitalism and the Ambivalent Legacy of Psychoanalysis." *New Left Review* 223 (May-June 1997): 69-89.

----------. "Trauma and Dereification: September 11 and the Problem of Ontological Security." *Constellations* 1 (2002): 98-105.

Žižek, Slavoj. *Looking Awry: An Introduction to Jacques Lacan through Popular Culture.* Cambridge: MIT Press, 1991.

----------. "Multiculturalism, or the Cultural Logic of Multinational Capitalism." *New Left Review* 225 (September-October 1997):28-51.

----------. *Welcome to the Desert of the Real!* London and New York: Verso, 2002.

***ibidem*-Verlag**

Melchiorstr. 15

D-70439 Stuttgart

info@ibidem-verlag.de

www.ibidem-verlag.de
www.ibidem.eu
www.edition-noema.de
www.autorenbetreuung.de

www.ingramcontent.com/pod-product-compliance
Lightning Source LLC
Chambersburg PA
CBHW071940240426
43669CB00048B/2463